CELEBRATIONS

Stylish Food & Decorating Ideas

JO SEAGAR & FIONNA HILL

photographs by

Jae Frew & John Daley

RANDOM HOUSE
NEW ZEALAND

All the photographs in the book are by Jae Frew
except the following taken by John Daley:
pages 2, 8, 48-49, 50, 51, 52-53, 58, 59, 63, 64,
79, 86, 87, 94, 100, 103, 111, 134, 193 and 196.
Photograph styling by Fionna Hill.

A RANDOM HOUSE BOOK
published by
Random House New Zealand
18 Poland Road, Glenfield, Auckland, New Zealand
www.randomhouse.co.nz

First published 2001

ISBN 1 86941 488 8

Internal design: Christine Hansen
Internal layout: Graeme Leather
Printed in New Zealand by Spectrum Print, Christchurch

CONTENTS

For my sister Shirley
— my faithful forager
Fionna

For Darling Rosso
— it wouldn't be a celebration without you
Jo

INTRODUCTION
JO SEAGAR

Throughout the year there are special dates in the calendar that unite families and bring friends together to celebrate an occasion. Some are ancient festivals and traditional feasting days, while others are simple get-togethers of good buddies and siblings to enjoy each other's company, count their blessings and mark an event. Many celebrations are linked to the seasons and reflect our rural history: when high days and holidays were dictated by such things as bringing in the harvest, surviving the dark days of winter and breaking the Lenten fast. Other celebrations are newly adopted customs and sometimes even straightforward excuses to party.

This book is about celebrating all kinds of occasions, it is about entertaining without pretensions. We hope it will become your inspirational resource book, full of fresh ideas, scrumptious, easy recipes and tips to take the stress out of your own special celebrations. Orchestrating a party, planning a theme, sending invitations, deciding what to wear, choosing the gifts and fitting into everyone's diary is hectic enough without adding culinary marathons to the list. So the food ideas and recipes are simple and easy to prepare. I've mixed old and new ideas with happy abandon – from sumptuously nostalgic dishes to new-wave fast-track food on the run.

The best news is that everything in *Celebrations*, the flowers, the settings, the wrappings, gifts and recipes are all extremely achievable – with lots of room for you to add your own special individual flourish.

Eat, drink and be merry, my friends.

FIONNA HILL

The vogue for flower arranging by prescription is over. As with Jo, maximum impact, minimum effort should be your rule of thumb when creating arrangements to complement your food. There's nothing like a wonderful background to set the mood, and it doesn't have to cost a fortune nor take all day. The important thing is to have fun. There's a bit of the creative in all of us. You don't have to be a top-notch florist to put together some wonderful decorative arrangements that will have your guests talking for weeks and marvelling at your skill. Keep up the ruse. Let them marvel!

Some of my ideas here require a little effort, but I'm especially keen to encourage you to think about colour, and to think outside the decorative square. Look for unusual bits and pieces. You might find them on the supermarket shelf or lying abandoned on the beach. Don't underestimate the wonder of foliage either. I use a wide selection of it and also many gathered materials. For me, nature in all its stages is one of my greatest sources of inspiration. Forget gypsophila and carnations!

Be bold in your endeavours: they need to stand out in the crowd of a roomful of people. Think big. Use arrangements to highlight the occasion's theme. If that is not appropriate, your designs should reflect the décor, accessories and nature of the celebration. Usually floral arrangements should complement the space rather than eclipse it.

Dining tables are an obvious focal point and can be covered with paper, simple inexpensive fabric or even leaves. The buffet or food serving area is another good spot. For immediate impact, wow your guests with an arrangement just inside the entrance. When guests are standing, keep arrangements near eye level so they won't be missed. A mantelpiece is often a great spot and a natural focal and congregating area.

Look for accessories and trims in unexpected low-cost places. Look in those craft and fabric emporiums, drapery, haberdashery and hardware shops, garden centres and children's toy shops. You'd be amazed at what you can put to good use!

And be a forager. Simple, artless, unsophisticated treasures from the countryside make for interesting and everlasting arrangements. And they usually last forever. Think cones, lichen, stones and seedheads.

The vegetable garden is another unlikely source of inspiration. What about those gorgeous burgundy beetroot stems, fiery chillies or the classic globe artichoke? Weeds and some so-called pests may be the thugs of the plant world, but they often have lovely leaves, flowers and seeds. The compost heap and the roadside could take on a whole different appeal. Fruit, too, is a great material to use in a floral design. Look at each growing thing for its intrinsic decorative qualities without thought for its conventional context.

Expect the unexpected in containers. You don't need a cupboard full of expensive vases. Brightly painted tin buckets are great for a party centrepiece. Many cooking containers like a lasagne dish, a rustic pottery terrine, ramekins or shot glasses make fun containers.

Candles add mood, on their own or incorporated with decorations. Their magic transforms the ordinary into extraordinary.

Above all, don't feel rule-bound. Adapt these ideas to suit your taste and style. Experiment. Enjoy.

NEW YEAR

By all means go for the traditional Western New Year celebrations of first footing, coal in hand, and plenty of whisky, but why not turn over a new leaf and look east instead?

The Asians have auspicious omens and wonderful symbols for a colourful alternative. Bring the Chinese New Year forward and invite over the neighbours for easy-to-prepare finger food and bubbly in an oriental-inspired setting.

The key to catering for a number is to have lots of just a handful of things – if the choice is too wide, guests want to try everything and end up with a hodge-podge of flavours on their plate, while you're too exhausted to join in the fun! And the fortune cookies are not just decorative – they can be eaten, too.

Red is the Chinese colour of luck and happiness: what better for New Year's Eve? Red, black and white coupled with Asian good fortune symbols make for a sophisticated New Year's Eve drinks party. Candles are placed on square ceramic plates and trimmed with a few black stones. The serving plates are square, in keeping with the minimal Asian theme. I found the fan in a craft and fabric emporium.

ABOVE: *These huge glass goblets on stems transform into impressive vases. The mass of red flowers is stunning and the clean straight stems look good through the glass. (Take care never to put scrappy stems or foliage under water in a glass container. In fact, always clean the stems of any foliage that will be below water level – the water will stay cleaner and your flowers will last longer.) The goblet on the right has two brick-sized blocks of wet floral foam in it. Pack some green moss inside the glass to hide the ugly foam. You could use stones but be careful that they do not scratch the glass. Top up*

with water. I've used a combination of real and artificial materials. The tall black grasses are artificial, the feathers are three extravagant real feather dusters and the fresh flowers are five heliconia blooms and five stems of leucadendron (I bought these with their heads already dipped in red wax). Choose odd numbers of materials that will be dominant (such as these red flowers). If you use only a few items, odd numbers are more pleasing to the eye. The goblet necks are tied with a red satin ribbon and black and red tassels.

RIGHT: *Each napkin (see previous page) has a gift of a Chinese red money envelope (right) with gold-wrapped chocolate coins for each guest. Fortune cookies are fun. This group of good luck symbols also includes a Japanese Daruma doll and fortune sticks.*

WASABI ASPARAGUS ROLLS

MAKES 30

1 teaspoon wasabi paste
soft butter or margarine to spread
30 slices sandwich-cut soft brown
   grainy bread
30 asparagus spears, cooked or
   canned
salt and freshly ground black
   pepper

Mix the wasabi and butter or margarine. Butter the bread, cut off the crusts, lay a spear of asparagus diagonally across each and roll up from one corner.

PASTRY CASES

Pastry cases can be bought pre-made and cooked from delicatessens or supermarkets. Or, buy sheets of frozen, pre-rolled pastry (savoury or sweet depending on your choice of filling). Cut out circles of the pastry with a cookie cutter and press into mini muffin tins. If you have one, place an identical tin on top of the pastry and put in the oven upside-down. This will stop the pastry from bubbling up as you want maximum room for your tasty fillings. If you don't have another tin, screw up balls of tinfoil and place inside the pastry. Bake in the oven at 130°C for 8-10 minutes. Remove the top tin or foil balls and continue to bake until the pastry has just coloured and is dry. Cool on a wire rack and store in airtight containers until used. They require no further baking but can be reheated if required.

SUSHI STACKS

MAKES APPROX 25

2¾ cups sushi rice, well rinsed
3 cups cold water
2 teaspoons salt
100 ml rice wine vinegar
1 tablespoon caster sugar
5 Nori (dried seaweed) sheets
wasabi-flavoured soy sauce
pink pickled ginger slices

Combine the rice and water in a saucepan and bring to the boil. Simmer uncovered without stirring for 8 minutes. Cover, turn off the heat and stand for 25 minutes, then fluff it up with a fork. Stir together the salt, rice wine vinegar and caster sugar. Sprinkle over the rice and mix with a fork. Cool. Place 1 sheet of Nori shiny side down on a board. Spread quarter of the rice over, cover with a second layer of Nori, then more rice, and continue stacking to end with a Nori sheet on top. Cut into squares with a very sharp knife, wetting the knife between each cut. Serve with wasabi-flavoured soy sauce and pink pickled ginger slices.

> **Tips:** Slices of smoked salmon or chives, smoked fish, prawns, etc can be added to the layers. The specialist ingredients in this recipe are available in Asian food stores or the Asian section of the supermarket.

OPPOSITE PAGE: *Caviar (red lumpfish roe) with sour cream in pastry cases (top right), sushi stacks (below left) together with asparagus rolls make a superb tower of nibbles for a New Year's drinks party.*

VALENTINE'S DAY

Here are two approaches for celebrating 14 February. The first is a sophisticated modern-style cocktail party for singles, letting oysters and champagne set the mood. Secondly, we've set the table for a romantic dinner for two, calling upon the tried and true elements of red roses, heart shapes, candles and the lovers, Harlequin and Columbine.

Valentine's Day can be about sharing a meal with a loved one, but it's also about giving a token of your love. A box of heart-shaped chocolate intensity cakes or a basket of chocolate-dipped cherries are just as impressive as an expensive gift from a shop. As shown, you can give the traditional bouquet a unique touch with a trimming as simple as feathers, while the presentation of a special gift can transform it into something that will be remembered for ever.

Oysters and champagne: the classic aphrodisiacs! The colours have been kept crisp and cool – grey, black, and white.

SERVING OYSTERS

Pick your oysters carefully – they should smell fresh and not be slimy. They won't keep long, though you can freeze them on the half shell – thaw them just before eating in fresh salted water. Oysters don't need to be cooked and can be eaten just as they are, raw, or you can serve them with a whole range of dressings: lemon juice and freshly ground black pepper; butter and toasted breadcrumbs; an oriental dressing of soy sauce, ginger, chopped spring onion and rice vinegar; a blob of sour cream and red caviar; or Dijon mustard mixed with sour cream. Even just a sprig of a green herb, such as dill or parsley, or a wedge of yellow lemon will provide a touch of eye appeal. Serve with hunks of bread to soak up the juices, such as the Irish Soda Bread (page 127) or my signature Beer Bread (page 181).

You can make the fascinating candle-holder by gluing (a hot-glue gun is the best, or use PVA) a few empty cleaned oyster shells to a metal six-candle holder (see store cupboard page 184). Heap more shells in the centre and around the edge once the candle-holder is in place in a simple bowl. Black candles add a sophisticated touch. The elegant raised glass bowl has just three fresh white anthuriums set among a few lovely veined leaves of Arum italicum. *The napkin-holders I made myself, using some light grey cardboard and cut-out hearts.*

CHERRIES DIPPED IN CHOCOLATE

2 cups chocolate melts or chopped dark chocolate
50 cherries with stalks attached

Melt chocolate in a bowl over a saucepan of hot water, being careful the water doesn't touch the bowl or, alternatively, melt chocolate in the microwave (see page 26). Dip the clean, dry cherries in the chocolate to half cover them. Allow to set on a piece of non-stick baking paper or tinfoil. Do not store in the fridge as the chocolate tends to sweat. These will keep for 1–2 days in a cool place.

*R*ed roses, the flowers of Venus, are the traditional symbol of love. In this leaf-edged bouquet the roses (aptly named 'Passion') are given a dashing twist with a few striking black feathers from a feather duster and swirls of bare silver birch twigs. They are tied with glamorous burgundy and black shot ribbon.

This is a wonderful presentation for both men and women. I've used salal leaves: this is an imported market foliage but you're bound to have something suitable in the garden. The birch is easily accessible and feathers can be bought in packets – or the bigger ones as singles – at some craft and fabric emporiums.

In a touch of theatre, Harlequin surveys a romantic table for two. Twenty fresh red roses (again, I've used 'Passion') are arranged in wet floral foam in a classic black iron urn encased in looped trails of ivy. Dried red roses are clustered in smaller iron urns and trimmed with gold cord and beaded gold hearts. The Harlequin and Columbine marionettes become quaint napkin trimmings.

HEART-SHAPED CROUTONS

toast bread
garlic salt
olive oil spray

Preheat the oven to 200°C. Using a heart-shaped cookie cutter press out heart shapes from a slice of toast bread. Sprinkle with garlic salt, spray with olive oil and bake for 8–10 minutes until crisp and golden. Toss a salad with your favourite dressing and sprinkle the heart-shaped croutons through it.

LEMON DILL CHICKEN

SERVES 2

1 tablespoon oil
2 single boneless and skinless chicken breasts
$1/2$ cup white wine or chicken stock
1 tablespoon chopped fresh dill (or $1/2$ teaspoon dried dill tips)
juice and grated rind of 1 medium sized lemon
$1/2$ teaspoon lemon pepper seasoning
1 spring onion, sliced

Heat oil in a large, preferably non-stick, pan over medium-high heat. Cook the chicken about 6–7 minutes, turning until light golden brown. Mix wine, dill, lemon juice and grated rind and lemon pepper seasoning. Pour over the chicken. Heat to boiling then reduce heat and simmer for 15 minutes. Remove chicken and boil the sauce for 3–4 minutes to reduce it by half. Pour over chicken breasts and sprinkle with sliced spring onions. Serve with rice.

HEART-SHAPED CHOCOLATE INTENSITY CAKES

MAKES 8–10 HEART CAKES

375 g (1 packet) dark chocolate melts
200 g butter
2 cups sugar
3 eggs
1 teaspoon vanilla essence
1 cup flour

Preheat the oven to 180°C. Melt the chocolate and butter together in the microwave or over a gentle heat and stir until smooth. In a food processor or using an electric mixer, mix together the sugar, eggs and vanilla. Add the melted chocolate mixture to this, stir until smooth and add the flour. Mix well. Pour into a baking-paper-lined 20 x 30 cm sponge-roll tin and bake for 35–40 minutes. Cool in the pan, then press out heart shapes with a cookie cutter or cut into wedges. Serve with Chocolate Fudge Sauce.

CHOCOLATE FUDGE SAUCE

375 g (1 packet) chocolate melts
300 ml cream

Melt the chocolate and cream together, stirring until combined. This sauce needs to be served warm as it sets solid at room temperature. It will keep in the fridge for 3 weeks.

> **Tip:** To melt chocolate, chop into pieces or use chocolate melts. Place in a bowl and either microwave in bursts of 30 seconds on medium or half power, stirring between bursts until melted and smooth, or place bowl over a saucepan of barely simmering water and stir until melted and smooth.

TOP LEFT AND RIGHT: *Harlequin is a sprite supposed to be invisible to all eyes but those of his faithful sweetheart Columbine. His task is to dance around the world (great job) to foil the roguish tricks of the Clown, who is also supposed to be in love with Columbine. This charming pair becomes unique napkin decorations.*

BOTTOM LEFT: *The heart of the matter: here a chunky burgundy heart-shaped candle makes a lovely long-lasting gift in a chintz-covered box, trimmed with fresh mini pink rosebuds.*

BOTTOM RIGHT: *Dried roses are an everlasting gift of love, and not just for Valentine's Day. You can find dried roses at some florists or dry your own by hanging bunches upside-down for several weeks. I've arranged these in dry floral foam inside a heart-shaped cardboard box and edged them with dried moss (both obtainable from florists or discount stores). The outside walls of the box have been glued (I used a hot-glue gun) with sticks of real cinnamon (from your supermarket or health food shop) and the box lid glued completely with moss.*

EASTER

Say the word Easter and most people will think of eggs, Hot Cross Buns and maybe Simnel Cake. In the northern hemisphere Easter celebrations mark the changing of the season to spring. It is a time of both rebirth and renewal – hence the use of eggs as an Easter symbol.

The flowers are spring bulbs and the colours of yellow and blue dominate. Not so here, but we have taken some traditional elements and given them a twist to suit our season. Our decorative ideas and simple recipes ensure you still deliver the essentials and have fun in the process.

Eggs are undervalued as ornaments. A pagan symbol of life's renewal, they can be used in a bowl on their own or in designs combined with many other materials such as moss, twigs and flowers. I have gathered eggs all my life and used some in this wonderful array. Here we have artificial eggs, onion skin-dyed real eggs and two types of edible eggs to make at home. (See page 33 for recipes.) The artificial eggs are hand-painted wood, polystyrene, stone and marble. The cluster at the bottom right-hand side is dyed with onion skin. They would make a lovely gift in a tiny straw-lined willow basket. Children can have lots of fun dying them. (See page 39 for the recipe.)

SUGAR DOUGH FONDANT
FOR SOFT EASTER EGGS

MAKES 6–8 SMALL EGGS

3 cups icing sugar
¾ cup cornflour
½ cup water
1½ tablespoons powdered gelatine
1 teaspoon cream of tartar
food colouring

Sift and mix the icing sugar and cornflour in a medium-sized bowl and put aside. Mix the water, gelatine and cream of tartar in a glass measuring jug. Allow to stand for 5 minutes. Heat the gelatine mixture on low in the microwave for 10-second bursts until the gelatine has dissolved. (Don't overheat it or the gelatine will lose its elasticity.) Stir into the icing sugar and cornflour and mix until well combined. Mix in a drop or two of food colouring to your desired colour. Place in an airtight container and refrigerate for 6–8 hours before using. Mould into egg shapes and allow to harden uncovered. If you flick food colouring onto the eggs with a paintbrush they look like finely speckled birds' eggs.

> **Tip:** This dough is best made with a cake mixer. It can be frozen for 6–8 weeks.

CHOCOLATE-COVERED EASTER EGGS

You can dip fondant eggs or bought marshmallow Easter eggs in chocolate for a luxury finish. Alternatively, you can follow a recipe for truffles (pages 101 or 121) and shape the mixture into eggs rather than round balls and then dip into the melted chocolate. Use chocolate melts, 1 packet (375 g) should easily dip 12–15 small eggs. Follow package instructions to melt in either the microwave or over a saucepan of hot water (see page 26). Milk or dark chocolate can be used. Use a little contrasting chocolate spooned into a small zip-lock plastic bag as a piping bag, to write names and personalise eggs.

HOT CROSS BUNS

MAKES 30

15 g dried yeast (2 sachets)
1¼ cups warm water
2 teaspoons sugar
3½ cups white flour
3½ cups wholemeal flour
2 teaspoons salt
¼ cup caster sugar
¾ cup raisins

½ cup sultanas or currants
75 g chopped peel
2 tablespoons cinnamon
2 tablespoons mixed spice
500 ml warm milk
75 g butter, melted
1 egg, beaten

CROSSES

¾ cup flour
¾ cup water

GLAZE

¼ cup sugar
2 tablespoons water

In a bowl combine the yeast, warm water and sugar. Leave in a warm place until the mixture becomes frothy (about 10 minutes). In a large bowl combine all the dry ingredients, including the fruit. Make a well in the middle and add the milk, melted butter, egg and the yeast mixture. Mix all the ingredients together and tip the dough onto a floured surface. Knead for at least 10 minutes (200 times!). Divide the dough into 30 pieces and roll into buns. Place them on a baking tray, cover with a tea-towel and leave in a warm place until the buns have doubled in size (about 1 hour). Make the crosses by combining the flour and water in a small bowl and mix to a paste. Stir until smooth. Put the paste into a piping bag with a small plain tube and pipe crosses onto the buns after they have risen. Bake at 220°C for 20 minutes. While they are cooking make the glaze by mixing the sugar and water until the sugar has dissolved. Remove the cooked buns from the oven and brush over with the glaze. Cool on a wire rack.

This charming Easter table decoration is set in a long black wooden tray. You could use a bread basket or even a pottery oven dish. Fill the container with a carpet of fresh moss – don't be too neat about it. Dampen it now and again. Cut succulents (easy to gather along the roadside here and there – without trespassing!) and sprigs of blue hydrangea. Place at intervals among discarded nests and artificial eggs in tones of soft watery blues and greens. These types of decorations are available at accessory or lifestyle shops and are worth snapping up when you see them. Sprigs of alder and lichen-encrusted twigs add a touch of the forest. Use more fresh flowers if you want. To keep these alive, you'll need to hide plugs of wet floral foam underneath the moss in which to spike the flowers. Candles could be popped in at intervals, too, for some Easter extravagance.

EASTER SIMNEL CAKE

1 cup blanched almonds	1 teaspoon baking soda
1 kg mixed dried fruit	$\frac{1}{4}$ cup golden syrup
$\frac{3}{4}$ cup brandy (or fruit juice)	$\frac{1}{2}$ cup milk
200 g butter, softened	3 eggs
1$\frac{1}{4}$ cups sugar	2 teaspoons vanilla
2 cups flour	2 teaspoons mixed spice

Place the almonds, mixed fruit and brandy or fruit juice in a microwave-safe bowl. Stir well and microwave on high for 4–5 minutes to warm it through. Stir and cover with clingfilm or a clean tea-towel and rest for at least 2 hours (or overnight). Beat the butter and sugar together. Stir in the fruit mixture, then add all the other ingredients. Mix well. Spoon into a well-greased and baking-paper-lined round 20 cm cake tin. Wrap the outside of the tin in several layers of newspaper to insulate the tin, leaving the top uncovered. Bake at 150°C for $2\frac{1}{4}$–$2\frac{1}{2}$ hours, until a skewer inserted into the centre comes out clean. Cool in the tin.

MARZIPAN DECORATION

Roll some almond marzipan into a circle 5 mm thick. Spread this over the cake, trimming to fit the top exactly. Roll the trimmings into 11 small balls and press these on top. Traditionally each represents one of the 11 apostles (excluding Judas).

OPPOSITE PAGE: *Huge ostrich eggs are available now that the giant birds are farmed. These eggs are blown. They look stunning inside a wire basket, which has six candle-holders attached, and tall rich cream tapers. The basket has been entwined with twigs to give it an untidy nest-like appearance, but overall a touch of Easter elegance.*

ONION-SKIN DYED EGGS

Fresh white eggs are best for this. Make sure they are clean and free from grease. Peel the brown outer skins from some onions and wrap several onion skins around each egg. Secure in place with two or more rubber bands. Cover the eggs with cold water in a saucepan and add a few drops of vinegar to make the colour more luminous. Simmer gently for about 30 minutes. Cool the eggs in the liquid, then carefully remove them and the rubber bands and onion skins. Let the eggs dry. Rub with a little salad oil or spray with clear varnish to deepen the colour and add lustre to the surface.

Other vegetable dyes for eggs:
- Yellow: saffron, turmeric, alder bark, caraway seeds.
- Black: pussy willow, alder bark.
- Red: beetroot juice.
- Blue: mallow, logwood.
- Green: spinach, nettle roots and leaves, young alder bark.
- Brown: alder bark.

TOP LEFT: *These beautiful little candles are in the shape of chocolate eggs, complete with yolks. They make an enchanting addition to the Easter table and could be set among flower heads and twigs. You can see from this photo that I rather like them in an egg carton. As Jo would say, easy peasy!*

TOP RIGHT: *A fun way to name a table place for an Easter guest is to write the name on an artificial (or hard-boiled real) egg in a little nest. It can then be a memento to take home. You'll have to hunt around gift shops for the little nests. They're the sort of relatively inexpensive treasure you need to buy when you see them and tuck away for later use.*

BOTTOM LEFT: *Soaps in the shape of eggs make an Easter gift with a difference for those watching calories. They are placed here in hand-made straw nests. The egg-paper wrapped parcel is trimmed with a tiny nest of eggs and a straw bird to continue the Easter egg theme, and tied with chocolate-brown jute.*

BOTTOM RIGHT: *Feather-covered decorative eggs in rich natural colours give an instant effect and make lovely accessories to fill a rustic container.*

MOTHER'S DAY

Something as easy to give as breakfast in bed means a lot to an overworked mum – or someone who is your mother in all but name.

With today's busy lifestyles, it's very rare to find time to spend lounging in bed. Nothing is nicer than waking to the smell of coffee rather than the blare of the alarm clock. Sunday papers, a stack of favourite, new, glossy magazines and a beautifully set tray are simple gestures that will make her feel special. Just as the presentation of the breakfast adds to the event, make sure the kitchen is left presentable, too! But if you're not on the spot, something you've made yourself – be it a freshly gathered tussie mussie or chocolate rum balls – will show you care.

Flowers are one of the oldest and most traditional gifts to give on any occasion. This simple posy for mother is made in the same way as the tussie mussie on page 45. Two bunches of white flowers are the only bought materials in it, the remainder are garden-picked snippets including euphorbia, variegated thyme, scented geranium and two long loops of fine ivy over the top of the posy. It is edged with a collar of large leaves. Two sheets of checked gingham tissue paper wrap it and it is tied with a gorgeous off-white velvet ribbon.

LEMON BLUEBERRY MUFFINS

MAKES 12

juice and grated rind of 2 lemons
4 teaspoons baking powder
2 cups flour
1½ cups milk
½ cup caster sugar
1 egg
¼ cup oil
1 large cup blueberries (if using frozen do not defrost)

Preheat the oven to 200°C. Mix all ingredients in a bowl. Don't overmix, but just combine the ingredients lightly. Spoon into well-greased deep muffin tins and bake for 15–18 minutes until the muffins spring back when lightly pressed.

Dust with icing sugar and serve warm.

WAFFLES

MAKES 8

3 eggs, separated
1½ cups milk
100 g butter, melted
2 tablespoons caster sugar
2 cups self-raising flour
1 teaspoon vanilla
oil spray or extra butter for greasing waffle iron

In a food processor or large bowl mix the egg yolks, milk, melted butter, caster sugar, flour and vanilla to a smooth batter. In another bowl beat the egg whites until stiff peaks form, then fold carefully into the batter.

Spray or brush a heated waffle iron with melted butter, spoon in 2–3 tablespoons of batter and cook until crisp and golden brown. Serve warm with whipped cream, maple syrup, fresh fruit and crispy bacon.

CRISPY BACON

I find my microwave on 'Crisp' function is the best way to cook delicious bacon. I use strips of streaky bacon. In a standard microwave you achieve the best crispiness if you cook the strips between two paper towels on high. To cook a large amount of bacon for 4 or more people it's best to do it in a hot oven with the bacon spread out on an oven tray with sides. Approximately 20 minutes at 200°C, turning once and draining well, does the trick.

*T*reat your mother to a breakfast tray laden with Lemon Blueberry Muffins (above) and Waffles served with Crispy Bacon, her favourite fruit and an egg (right). Serve with a special fruit juice or make your own drink such as those on pages 72, 172 and 173.

Historically, the tussie mussie was a nosegay of selected scented herbs, sometimes interspersed with flowers, to combat the unpleasant odours of bad sanitation and to fight off plague germs. Luckily, times have changed and now it's a lovely way to express sentiments through the language of flowers. Choose flowers and leaves with meanings to express your feelings, and add a card with the bouquet.

This lovely tussie mussie is made of garden snippets in late autumn, when, at a glance, there seems little to pick. But remember, even the smallest sprigs add

charm to a small posy. Here I've used forget-me-nots for true love, mimosa for sensitivity, angelica for inspiration, parsley for festivity, rosemary for remembrance, ivy for friendship, nutmeg geranium for an expected meeting, box for stoicism and roses for love. I have taken the liberty of using some extra flowers with unknown meanings. But, a word of warning: I discarded lavender and hydrangea from my posy when I found they can mean distrust and heartlessness in some versions of language of flowers!

Have a rubber band ready because

you can't put the posy down until it is complete. Begin with tall spiky snippets at the centre, place some of the large blooms in next and keep turning the posy and building on it with different flowers and a few leaves. Keep most of the leaves for the outer edge as protection and a collar. Here nandina is lovely for the final layer as it curves downwards.

Tie or rubber-band the posy high up the stems to keep it firm. Cut the stems to the same length and remind your mum, mother-in-law or mentor to re-cut them before putting them into water. Finish with a lovely ribbon.

CHOCOLATE RUM BALLS

MAKES 40

375 g dark chocolate (or 1 packet dark chocolate melts)
100 g butter
2 cups raisins or sultanas
3 tablespoons rum or 2 teaspoons rum essence
2 cups icing sugar
1½ cups coconut to roll balls in

Melt the chocolate and butter together, mixing until smooth (see page 26 for tips on melting chocolate). Add the raisins, rum and icing sugar. The mixture should be quite stiff – if it is too soft to be rolled into little balls chill it for a while first. Roll the balls in coconut and store in the fridge in an airtight container. Serve chilled.

> **Tip:** The Rum Balls will keep for 3–4 weeks if refrigerated.

I sprayed a recycled cardboard box with bronze florist's spray to give it a sheen. Use chocolate organza ribbon (or any colour that takes your fancy) for the lid trimming and glue the loose ends inside the top of the box (so that it won't be spoiled when the gift is opened). Fill with Jo's Chocolate Rum Balls and tie a generous bow in the lid centre. The luscious rose is a hat decoration. A tiny book on chocolate transforms this little treasure into an unforgettable gift that will have them marvelling for years.

CHAPTER FIVE

WINTER SOLSTICE

The short, dark daylight hours were a time of low spirits, so this period was traditionally a time for celebration and anticipation of better days to come.

The Yule feast of the Norseman was celebrated in Northern Europe, with log fires to aid the ailing sun gods and sacred places decorated with holly and ivy. When the Roman emperor Constantine was converted to Christianity in the 4th century, he substituted Christian festivals for the pagan ones: it seemed an easier task than banning the Druid festivals completely. However, given Christmas arrives in the summer here, why not lighten those long winter nights and enact the solstice (21/22 June) with traditional customs of a winter festival?

This candelabra is magic and will transform your table in a flash. Don't be fooled by its initial bare look – this is its beauty. Dress up; pare down. It holds six elegant candles over a decorative base at a low enough level for dinner guests to see one another across the table. Flickering light from the stunning candelabra will set the scene for a memorable meal.

Soft grey-greens and blue complement the antique pewter chargers and sage green dinner plates. I first wound long, fine, bare silver birch branches along the candle-holder (see page 184 for a photograph of the unadorned holder). Have the finest tips at the outer end, working in towards the centre with thicker branches. Don't worry if fine tips stick out – they add interest and a natural look. The candle-holder is placed in a shallow plastic dish with a circle of wet

floral foam around the centre. The indigo blue candles are set firmly in the candelabra. Into the foam I stick long trails of ivy and sprays of cedar and larch. The succulents are placed near the centre. (Take care to leave the attractive powdery bloom on the succulent petals.) Long trails of soft lichen are wound through the arrangement. Two varieties of cones are arranged in groups throughout the design. For each diner bare silver birch twigs are wound into a circlet to hold a napkin. A sprig of rosemary adds a final festive touch.

There is no need to add flowers to this table centre. The muted greens create the feeling of a forest floor on this lovely old chestnut French farmhouse table. Adding brighter colours would be a mistake, and interfere with nature's ambience.

49

PANFORTE

¼ cup flour
½ cup cocoa
1 teaspoon ground cinnamon
1 cup blanched whole almonds
1 cup walnut halves
1 cup toasted hazelnuts, skins
  removed
½ cup mixed peel
1 teaspoon finely grated orange
  rind
1 teaspoon finely grated lemon
  rind
½ cup castor sugar
¼ cup honey
½ cup icing sugar, for dusting

PANFORTE CONTINUED

Preheat the oven to 160°C. Brush a shallow 20-cm round cake tin with oil, line and grease the base. Place flour, cocoa and cinnamon in a bowl. Add nuts, peel and rind, and stir. Place sugar and honey in a pan and stir over a low heat until the mixture boils and the sugar has dissolved. Reduce the heat and simmer, uncovered, without stirring for 5 minutes or until the syrup forms a soft ball when a few drops are placed in a glass of cold water. Pour the hot syrup onto the other mixture, and combine. Spoon into tin and spread quickly and evenly; bake for 30 minutes, remove from oven and leave to cool in tin. Turn the Panforte out onto aluminium foil and wrap well. Leave for 1-2 days before cutting. Dust heavily with icing sugar before cutting into thin wedges.

SMOKED SEAFOOD CHOWDER

SERVES 6

1 tablespoon butter
1 leek, finely sliced
1 medium onion, chopped
1 tablespoon flour
1 cup fish stock (use the liquid
  from the canned smoked fish)
2 cups milk
1 cup sweetcorn (fresh off the cob,
  frozen, canned or creamed)

1 potato, peeled and diced
310 g can smoked fish fillets or
  2 cups flaked smoked fish
2 cups (approx) mixed seafood
$\frac{1}{2}$ cup cream
$\frac{1}{2}$ cup chopped parsley
salt and freshly ground black
  pepper

Melt the butter in a large saucepan and add the leek and onion. Stir-fry for 3–4 minutes, then stir in the flour. Cook for another minute or two and pour in the fish stock and milk. Add the corn, diced potato, smoked fish and other seafood. Gently simmer until the potato is softened and the soup is smooth and thick. Finally, add the cream and parsley and season to taste with a little salt and pepper (note that smoked fish tends to be quite salty already).

This rich, chunky creation would grace any sideboard or coffee table for winter solstice celebrations. An old French copper cooking pan makes a stunning container for a floral arrangement. The hearty 'plaque d'office' is just right for this superb Georgian oak dresser and the rich green majolica plates enclose the design well and complement the traditional winter colours of rich red and green. I love using fruit in flower arrangements. Here it creates an abundant feel to this arrangement – these are tamarillos. The rose 'Black Beauty' gives a look of voluptuous, rich velvet. The deep green foliage includes bay, camellia, angelica and bronze-tinted nandina leaves and seeds. Lichen-covered twigs add interest and another texture. The chunky liver-coloured candle is the perfect centrepiece for this substantial arrangement. Triple wicks are great in such a large candle. Two blocks of wet floral foam are placed inside the pan. The candle is placed in next, then the short-cut foliage is arranged in groups. Tamarillos are each wired to create a false stem to anchor into the foam and the roses are the last addition. Some materials break the edge of the pan and others are clustered near the candle.

WARM MULLED WINE

SERVES 12

2 oranges
16 whole cloves
2 cups water
1 cup sugar
12 cinnamon sticks
peeled rind of an orange
2 x 750 ml bottles dry red wine
12 orange slices

Cut the oranges in half and stud the outsides with 4 cloves per half. Bring the water to the boil in a large, heavy (not aluminium) saucepan. Add the orange halves, sugar, cinnamon sticks and orange peel, and stir over a medium heat until the sugar dissolves. Simmer 5 minutes. Add the wine, adjust the heat so that the mixture is almost simmering and cook 20 minutes. Do not boil. Remove the orange halves, rind and cinnamon sticks from wine. Ladle the wine into 12 glasses or glass mugs and garnish with the used cinnamon sticks and an orange slice hooked onto the rim of each mug.

OPPOSITE PAGE: *For this side-table arrangement I have repeated the copper theme, using a copper kitchen mould. In the centre I've placed a plain metal six-candle holder (there are a variety of these in the shops), holding burgundy candles. Black would also look stunning, or you could go bright with orange. A block of wet floral foam is then placed in the centre. Trails of ivy, angelica and Arum italicum leaves (this is often regarded as a weed – as are many plants I like!) are spiked into the foam, along with alder cones and catkins. The bare branches and loops of silver birch mirror the cold, sparse, moody look of the winter landscape. Spike rich red tamarillos onto satay sticks and arrange into groups: I like odd numbers, in this instance three. I've added a few full-blown red roses. Clove oranges and bunched cinnamon sticks on the table top are the perfect companion for spicy mulled wine. The clove oranges last for years, and the tamarillos about two weeks.*

BABY PECAN PIES

MAKES 16

125 g butter	**60 g butter, melted**
1 cup flour	**1 egg**
½ cup icing sugar	**1 cup brown sugar**
1 cup pecan nuts	**1 teaspoon vanilla essence**

Place the 125 g butter with the flour and icing sugar in a food processor and run the machine until the pastry clumps together in a ball. Divide into 16 balls, then with floured hands press the pastry into the bases and up the sides of non-stick (or well-greased) mini muffin tins. Refrigerate for at least 30 minutes – the pastry will set quite firm, and you bake it from cold. Divide the pecans equally between the chilled pastry cases, breaking the nuts as required. Mix the melted butter, egg, brown sugar and vanilla until smooth and 'gluey' and spoon or pour carefully over the nuts. Do not overfill each little pie. Bake in a preheated 180°C oven for 20–25 minutes until the pastry is golden and crisp. Take out of the oven and leave in the mini muffin tins for a few minutes until the pies are cool enough to handle. Give each pie a little twist around to loosen the bottom, then carefully lift out to cool on a wire rack. These are delicious served warm and can be reheated easily and served with whipped cream or ice-cream.

OVEN-DRIED CARAMELISED PEARS

MAKES 24 SLICES

6 firm pears (without any bruising)
½ cup caster sugar
½ cup boiling water

Preheat the oven to 120°C fan bake. Cut each pear into 4 slices from stalk to bottom (as shown in picture). Leaving the pips and peel intact, discard (or eat) the 2 outer slices of each. Dissolve the caster sugar in the boiling water, then brush the pear slices on both sides with this syrup. Place them flat on a baking-paper-lined oven tray. Put them in the oven and set the timer for 30 minutes. After this time brush both sides of the pears again and cook the other side for a further 30 minutes. Repeat this process every 30 minutes for about 4 hours, until the pears are just dried out and go a lovely caramel crispy colour at the edges.

> **Tips:** Cooled and stored in an airtight container these make a wonderful gift or accompaniment to a cheese board or festive dessert or glazed ham. Apples can also be dried and caramelised in this fashion. I usually fill the oven with trays of sliced fruit to make the most of the long cooking time.

A simple cardboard bell is covered with leaves and tied with an oyster-coloured velvet ribbon, creating a rustic yet chic addition to lichen-covered twigs.

OPPOSITE PAGE: *A conventional cone-shaped object is covered with tiny dried leaves to create an attractive focal point. Set on a raised platter and surrounded by nuts, it quickly provides a simple side-table decoration.*

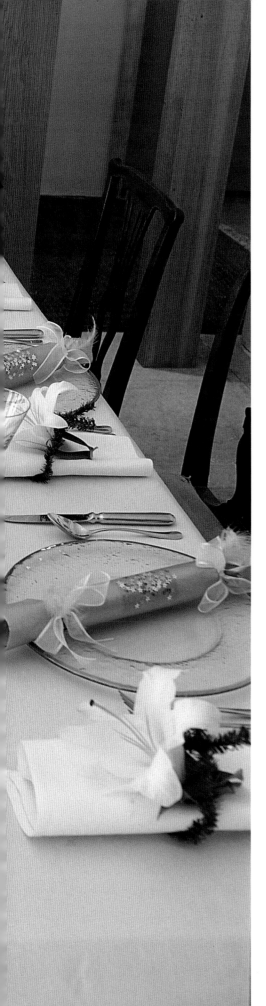

CHRISTMAS

In the second millennium, Christmas may mean different things to different people, but for most it involves sharing food and presents with loved ones.

This is a time for tradition – indeed, who hasn't felt teary-eyed if something that was part of past Christmases is missing? So, we've collected ideas for making these easier and more delicious. While tradition is important, it's refreshing to introduce new ideas as well. We've included some alternative approaches, added a touch of the modern and looked to the Pacific for new ways to mark this festivity that are more fitting to our summer season and the beginning of a time of relaxation and holiday for most.

This Christmas dinner setting is cool and icy, purposely designed for a Yuletide summer's day. At the centre is an artificial garland that would normally be used along a mantelpiece or over a door frame. It has been placed in a straight line down the table with the wired sprigs underneath tweaked to lie flat on the surface. An inexpensive long white feather boa has been twined along the garland, and wide silver grey organza ribbon makes generous bows along the length. Bought twig balls sprayed silver are placed at intervals, as are glistening white casablanca lilies. To keep them fresh, the lilies could be put into plastic water phials or even into tiny plugs of wet floral foam encased in plastic clingfilm and hidden in the greenery.

RIGHT: *M*inimal and magic. Lichen-covered branches hang with dusty silver baubles. Each is tied with a tiny piece of fine ice-blue ribbon. The branches are set in a contemporary zinc vase between triangles of shining silver mesh.

DOUBLE CHOCOLATE FUDGE BROWNIES

200 g butter
250 g dark chocolate melts or chips
2 cups caster sugar
4 eggs, beaten

1 teaspoon vanilla essence
¾ cup flour
¼ cup self-raising flour
½ cup cocoa

125 g (the rest of the bag) dark chocolate melts, chopped

Preheat the oven to 160°C. Line a 20 x 30 cm sponge-roll tin with baking paper. Melt the butter and 250 g chocolate together (see page 26). Beat the caster sugar, eggs and vanilla in the food processor or with a hand-held mixer. Add the melted chocolate mix, along with the flours and cocoa. Stir in the extra chopped chocolate. Pour into the prepared tin and bake for 50 minutes until firm. Cool in the tin and cut into small bars or chunks. When cold store in an airtight container. To serve, sieve icing sugar over to decorate.

LEFT: *These charming straw and wood angels are from Austria. Hanging on a bundle of roof thatching they create an evocative hint of Christmas. They bring back fond memories for me of an Austrian friend and her village just outside Vienna. Christl shared with me the ancient traditions of crafting simple but joyful decorations for this special time of the year, no matter where in the world you are.*

FOLLOWING PAGE: *Christmas in midsummer is a perfect setting for a Pacific theme. The huge tapa cloth hides two trestle tables and makes a natural textured cover. I gathered a few large exotic-looking leaves to put with the imported cerise ginger flowers and the stems of fascinating ornamental pink bananas. (You could use edible bananas, coconuts and mangoes with New Zealand-grown bird of paradise flowers.) I simply draped these in groups over an upturned wooden*

container to raise their level. A group of fat chocolate-coloured pillar candles are on hand for a meal that may go on after sunset. The natural oatmeal linen napkins are wrapped with a dried bamboo leaf (bought from an Asian food supply store). They're great for writing guests' names on too. Here I have trimmed them with a mini cymbidium orchid for each guest. All the serving bowls and dinnerware are in keeping with the Pacific theme.

MARINATED PACIFIC-STYLE SEAFOOD

SERVES 4–6

500 g fresh fish fillets, boned, skinned and thinly sliced
½ cup fresh lime juice
1 tablespoon grated lime peel
½ cup thick coconut cream
3 spring onions (or 1 small red onion), finely sliced
1 red chilli, deseeded and finely sliced
¼ cup chopped flat-leaf Italian parsley or coriander
salt and freshly ground black pepper
2 cups cooked seafood (eg baby shrimps, prawns, smoked baby
  mussels) or scallops (optional)
2–3 cups finely shredded or torn crispy salad leaves (eg cos or iceberg
  lettuce, celery leaves, watercress, pea sprouts)

Place the fish in a glass or china bowl. Mix through the lime juice and grated
rind. Cover and refrigerate for at least 2 hours. Drain off and discard any excess
juice and mix through the coconut cream, onion, chilli and parsley. Season
generously with salt and freshly ground black pepper to taste, and add the
optional seafood. Place a handful of crisp washed salad leaves on each plate and
divide the seafood between them. Garnish with fresh herbs and lime wedges and
serve with a fork or chopsticks.

> **Tip:** A clean clam or paua shell makes a great serving dish.

CHILLI FISH FRITTERS

3 eggs
1 cup self-raising flour
salt and freshly ground black pepper
$\frac{1}{2}$ cup ginger ale or water
2 cups flaked or finely chopped cooked fish
1 cup sweetcorn kernels
$\frac{3}{4}$ cup desiccated coconut (preferably the coarse-cut)
3 tablespoons chopped fresh coriander
2–3 tablespoons sweet chilli sauce
oil for frying

Mix the eggs, self-raising flour, salt, pepper and ginger ale to a smooth consistency, then stir in the next five ingredients. Heat the oil in a large frying pan over a medium-high heat. Cook 4–5 spoonfuls of mixture at a time until golden brown on both sides and cooked through. Serve with extra sweet chilli sauce.

Tip: These can be made in advance and reheated in the oven.

BOTTOM LEFT: *Dried leaves (bought from an Asian food supply store) make simple place names. I have written the names in black felt pen, folded the bottom of the leaf and stapled it into a cone shape and popped in a conical shell for decoration. A flower head would be a pretty alternative in the cone.*

TOP RIGHT: *Dried pandanas leaf (flax would work too) is circled and stapled to hold a cone-shaped folded napkin. I used sheet music that I had reduced (on a photocopier) to fit half an A4 page and printed onto craft paper. The sensational seafood menu is written on the reverse.*

TOP LEFT: *Paua shells hold what is known as 'candle sand' – essentially fine grains of wax and a wick. Remember to put sellotape along the tiny row of holes in the shell before pouring in the fine grains. Small tea-light candles would also look good set in sand inside the shells.*

BOTTOM RIGHT: *You can almost hear the lapping water when you look at this 'candlescape'. Tapa cloth makes a natural textured background. I stood the candles on some bark just in case they dripped. While scouring the seashore I found this rusty old chain which I've woven around the candles (driftwood or clean seaweed would work too). You'd be amazed at the treasures you can unearth while beachcombing. Gather and keep anything you find! Place a few polished stones (or shells) and woven cane balls randomly around the setting. Woven raffia boxes are decorated with seagrass stars. You could pop some flower heads such as hibiscus among this scene, but I enjoyed keeping it to earthy colours. The manufactured items came from lifestyle and craft stores; the stars from Trade Aid.*

LEMON SQUASH

MAKES 3 LITRES OF CORDIAL

6 lemons
1.5 kg sugar
50 g (¹/₂ packet) citric acid
boiling water

Peel the rind off 2 of the lemons with a potato peeler, taking care not to get any pith. Place the peel and 2 cups of the sugar in the food processor and run the processor until the rind is really ground up and the sugar is yellow and oily looking. Squeeze all 6 lemons and mix the juice with the lemon sugar. Add the remaining sugar and the citric acid, then enough boiling water to make the volume up to 3 litres. Stir until the sugar has dissolved. Cool and store in the fridge. To serve, dilute with cold water.

COCONUT ICE

100 g butter
1 cup milk
6 cups icing sugar
1 teaspoon salt
1 cup desiccated coconut
2 teaspoons coconut essence

Place the butter, milk, icing sugar and salt in a medium-sized saucepan and heat gently until the sugar dissolves. Bring the mixture to the boil and keep the heat sufficient to just maintain the boil, stirring only occasionally, until the mixture reaches soft-ball stage (120°C). Add the coconut and coconut essence and remove from the heat. Cool for 5–10 minutes, then beat until the mixture thickens. Pour into a greased tin approximately 20 x 20 cm. Allow to cool and cut into squares. Add a drop of food colouring with the coconut if you like.

COCONUT SORBET

MAKES 1 LITRE

1 cup warm water
1 cup sugar
2 cups coconut milk

1 teaspoon coconut essence
$\frac{1}{2}$ cup desiccated coconut
2 egg whites, stiffly beaten

Dissolve the sugar in the water and cool. Mix into this sugar syrup the coconut milk, coconut essence and coconut. Freeze in shallow container for at least 8 hours. An hour before serving, scoop the frozen mixture into a food processor bowl. Add the beaten egg whites and blend until the mixture is fluffy and white. Refreeze for at least 1 hour to firm.

Tip: This sorbet can be prepared ahead up to the first freezing stage. Cleaned shells make a superb bowl for a scoop of Coconut Sorbet.

LEFT: *All the parcels are kept in the same Pacific theme with woven flax and raffia boxes, hand-made paper, seagrass and pandanas leaf ties, and dried seed trims.*

BELOW: *Coconut Ice. (See recipe page 72.)*

OPPOSITE PAGE: *This traditional artificial fir tree has been given a touch of the Pacific to make a lovely summertime Christmas tree. The metal base has been disguised inside a cut woven bag. Exotic shells and huge starfish, small woven ketes and tufts of feathers make interesting natural decorations. The shells and starfish have short lengths of florist's wire glued to them (with a hot-glue gun or PVA) to fasten them to the branches. The feathers are clustered together and wired by making a hairpin shape and tightly binding one end of the wire around the feather ends and around the other end of the wire. The wire hoop is then hooked around a tree branch. Don't be tempted to add bows or metallic glitz. Keep it simple and true to theme.*

GARLIC, LIME MAYONNAISE DIP FOR SEAFOOD

MAKES 3 CUPS

2 teaspoon salt
1 teaspoon finely ground white pepper
grated rind 6 limes
½ cup fresh lime juice
6 egg yolks
2–3 cloves garlic (1 teaspoon crushed)
2 cups light olive, grapeseed or canola oil
¼–½ cup boiling water
3 tablespoons finely chopped dill or parsley
3 kaffir lime leaves, finely shredded (optional)

Place salt and pepper, grated rind and lime juice, egg yolks and garlic in a food processor and blend to combine. With the motor running very slowly, drizzle in a thin stream of oil. A thick pale mayonnaise will form. Occasionally scrape down the sides of the bowl and don't be too impatient to add the oil too quickly as the mayonnaise could curdle. Add enough boiling water to thin the mayonnaise to dressing consistency. Add the chopped dill or parsley and optional shredded kaffer lime leaves. Store covered in the fridge. This will keep for up to 2 weeks.

CURRIED CHICKEN AND MANGO SALAD

SERVES 4–6

1 large onion, roughly chopped
1 tablespoon tomato purée
2 teaspoons curry powder
1 cup chicken stock
1 cup red wine
1½ cups prepared mayonnaise
3 tablespoons soft or runny apricot jam
300 ml cream, thickly whipped
3–4 cups sliced cooked chicken
large bunch grapes (about 2 cups)
2 mangoes, peeled, stoned and cut into bite-sized pieces
½ cup chopped parsley or coriander

Simmer the chopped onion, tomato purée, curry powder, chicken stock and red wine for 30 minutes until well reduced to a chutney-like consistency. Remove from the heat. When the mixture is cold, fold in the mayonnaise, apricot jam and whipped cream. Mix in the chicken, grapes and mango pieces, and spoon onto a large serving platter. Garnish with the chopped parsley or coriander.

*T*hese fresh patterned plaid napkins are tied with fine orange embroidery ribbon and trimmed with naïve clay Christmas tree decorations. Metallic trimmings would look out of place here.

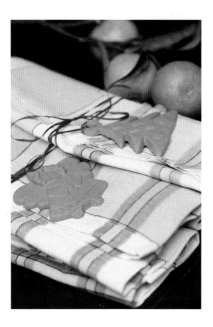

RIGHT: *I love having a theme for Christmas decorations. Picking up the seaside theme used earlier rings the changes while still looking festive. Shells have soft natural colours and wonderful textures. Simple shells gathered on any beach, such as the scallops here, are as suitable as more exotic examples. I have added a touch of glitter to the edges of the scallop shells to provide a festive touch.*

Not wishing to exaggerate my tampering with them I chose a fine burnished bronze glitter to delicately edge the shells. The wreath is off the shelf from a Christmas supply shop. Shells are wired at their base and attached to the wreath among the pine sprigs. Two looped ribbons end in a voluptuous bow at the top. The platter of exotic shells beneath the wreath is a lovely addition to the setting.

CITRUS, VANILLA & CLOVE GLAZED HAM

- 1 large ham (buy a pre-cooked ham on the bone with skin attached)
- 1 packet (approx 100) whole dried cloves
- 2 cups orange marmalade
- 1 teaspoon vanilla essence
- ¼ cup orange juice (bottled is fine)

Remove the leathery outer layer of skin from the ham by making an insertion with a sharp knife, then sliding your hands under the skin and peeling it off. It's surprisingly easy to do. (Leave the white fatty layer in place.) Press the cloves into the fatty layer all over the ham – you can make patterns or rows of cloves or just press them in at random. Heat the marmalade, vanilla and orange juice until the marmalade has melted and the mixture is good and runny. Sieve or strain out any solid bits of marmalade and generously brush the ham all over the surface with the syrup. Place the ham in a large roasting dish and bake for approximately 1½ hours at 180°C. Baste it frequently throughout this time and check that it does not start to scorch. The skin will take on a glorious golden brown glaze. Small sections that may be colouring up too fast can be covered with pieces of oiled tinfoil. To serve, decorate the bone end with fresh citrus or bay leaves or bunches of herbs and a pretty ribbon.

MUSTARD FRUITS

1 cup fruit chutney
1 cup apricot jam
1 cup mixed dried fruit (eg apple, apricot, raisins, peach, pineapple,
currants, crystallised ginger)
cold water to cover
1 cup brandy or orange juice
1 cinnamon stick
2 mandarins or small oranges, sliced (leave skin on)
1 tablespoon sweet chilli sauce
1 tablespoon wholegrain mustard

Mix together the fruit chutney and jam and put aside. Put the dried fruit in a small saucepan or microwave-safe bowl, cover with cold water, then add the brandy, cinnamon stick and mandarin slices. Simmer or microwave until nearly all the liquid has been absorbed and the fruit is syrupy and plump, adding extra water if required. Stir the chutney jam mixture into the fruit, along with the chilli sauce and mustard. Add a little extra brandy or water if it is too dry. Store sealed in clean sterilised jars or in a covered container in the fridge.

> **Tip:** Keeps for up to 2 months and makes a great gift or accompaniment to ham or Christmas poultry.

An orange pierced with cloves is often made for Christmas giving and is something children can readily help with. (Remember, patience is a virtue, especially at Christmas!) I've taken a short cut and used just a few cloves to create spicy decorative mandarins for a small raised glass dish. These are a bit of fun to complement the citrus theme of our Citrus, Vanilla & Clove Glazed Ham. Use firm mandarins, oranges or lemons and spike two rows of cloves going in opposite directions into the flesh, dividing the fruit into quarters with the rows. The gorgeous French ribbons add a sumptuous touch. Sadly, the fruit will probably last only a few days – but it's Christmas, after all.

ICE-CREAM CHRISTMAS PUDDING

SERVES 8–10

2 litres best-quality vanilla ice-cream
2 cups mixed dried fruit (I use a commercial mix of currants, ginger,
  raisins, peel, red and green glacé cherries)
½ cup extra mixed dried fruit
½ cup white chocolate, chopped finely (or chocolate chips)
1 tablespoon rum or brandy essence (optional)

Soften the ice-cream in the microwave or at room temperature until it's easily stirrable. Add the other ingredients and mix well. Pour into a plastic or tinfoil-lined pudding mould or basin and refreeze until solid. This can be done up to a month before you want to eat it. To serve, remove from the freezer and turn out onto a serving plate or dish. Unfortunately the flaming of the traditional Christmas pud doesn't work with the ice-cream one, but you could cheat and insert a small metal bottle top or eggcup of warmed brandy in the top of the pudding. As long as the brandy is warmed first it can be ignited for a brief glowing effect.

TROPICAL FRESH FRUIT SALAD WITH

LEMONGRASS SYRUP

2 cups sugar
2 cups water
4 tablespoons lemongrass stalks, crushed
chunky pieces of fruit (kiwifruit, melon, pawpaw, watermelon, grapes,
  pineapple, bananas, fresh or canned lychees, orange, mandarin
  segments, etc)

In a small saucepan dissolve the sugar in the water over a gentle heat. Add the crushed lemongrass stalks. (I find a jar of crushed lemongrass stalks, from the supermarket, an invaluable store cupboard item.) Simmer for 10 minutes, then allow to cool. Strain to remove the lemongrass stalks. Discard them and chill the syrup. Pour over the fruit, adding extra fruit juice as desired. This syrup keeps indefinitely in the fridge (see page 88 for photograph).

Rose petals are edible and therefore make a safe food trimming. This lovely striped garden bloom and a few rose hips make perfect decorations for Jo's ice-cream pudding. The bright orange-coloured enamel plate matches our citrus theme.

Gift wrapping to wow your friends! Hot pink and buttercup yellow really make a statement. Let your imagination run wild with non-traditional Christmas gift-wrapping. Think about colour co-ordinating all your wrappings and trimmings, right down to your cards, to create a sumptuous scene. Here the wraps are hand-made paper, crêpe paper, tulle, and striped giftwrap. The ties are gorgeous French ribbons, some plain and

some splendidly patterned and textured. A double row of ribbon sets off the top strip beautifully. Wire-edged ribbon is wonderful for making the bows sit up luxuriously and curve in any direction you choose. Use brightly coloured corrugated cardboard boxes to make simple commercially bought sweets, such as liquorice allsorts, look tempting. Feathers make extravagant-looking trims – buy pieces of feather boa and chop them

into sections. Some feathers I used singly and tied them to the ends of fine hot pink ribbon. The home preserves are pickled lemons, lemon curd and mustard. For a touch of fun I have covered them with circles of tulle, with a layer of crêpe paper underneath to disguise the jar tops. Gift cards are hand-made in matching colours.

86

THE FAMOUS NEW ZEALAND PAVLOVA

SERVES 6–8

**6 egg whites (at room
   temperature)**
2 cups caster sugar
1 teaspoon vanilla essence
1 teaspoon malt vinegar
2 teaspoons cornflour
whipped cream
sliced fresh fruit

Preheat the oven to low (110–120°C). In a large metal, porcelain or glass (not plastic) bowl beat the egg whites until soft peaks form. A hand-held electric beater is ideal for this job. Gradually, a teaspoon at a time, add the caster sugar. I emphasise – add the sugar slowly. The mixture should be getting glossy, thick and shiny with each addition, and the whole sugar-adding process should take at least 10 minutes. Beat in the vanilla, vinegar and cornflour. Spoon the mixture into a round, dinner-plate-sized mound on a baking tray covered with baking paper. Bake for 1½ hours. Cool, and serve topped with whipped cream and sliced fresh fruit.

To make the most of the decorative value of the Tropical Fresh Fruit Salad (recipe page 85), we've served it in a vase rather than a traditional bowl.

*F*resh apples on ribbons make a folksy decoration to hang on a tree, beneath a mantelpiece, or on a row of hooks as shown here. In our warm Christmas climate apples that have been pierced with wire will not last long before rotting. But don't they make a charming decoration even for a few days?

I suggest you make the ribbons all different lengths for a haphazard effect. I've used a fresh mint green and white gingham. The ribbon does not really go through the apple: it's a little sleight of hand. Move over, all you magicians! Use a length of strong florist's wire for each apple (about three times the height of your apple), and bend it in half like a hairpin. Spike both ends through the apple from the bottom and push up and out of the top, keeping the wires as

straight as possible. This will leave the hoop of the hairpin just sticking from the bottom and the two separate ends coming out either side of the stalk on the top.

Cut a small length of ribbon (about 10 cm) and thread this through the hoop of wire at the bottom of the apple, so the wire crosses the middle of the ribbon. Pull the two wire ends tight from the top of the apple. This will fold the ribbon in two and

bring the doubled end of it snugly up to the apple base looking as though the ribbon is coming out of it.

Use a much longer length of ribbon for the top. Fold it in two and position the fold where the apple stalk grows. Bend the wires coming out across the fold of ribbon, twisting a couple of times. Cut off any ugly wire ends, knot the ribbon over the twisted wire and hang up.

ABOVE: *Jute angels make an enchanting line-up for a row of pegs or under a mantelpiece. These are hanging on the prongs of an old wooden leaf rake.*

OPPOSITE PAGE: *The seeds of the flax plant create an unusual permanent Christmas tree with their natural conical shape. This tree is small enough for an apartment or a sideboard, but you could make a huge one with tall flax pod branches and set it in a large bucket.*

This design is kept in the natural colours of wood, stone and earth, which are great for our midsummer Christmas. Keep the decorations natural too, and resist the temptation to add traditional bows and metallic decorations. The tiny woven kete tree decorations here add a simple form and texture. Shells would be lovely too. (See the Christmas tree on page 74.)

I like the narrow conical-shaped container as it reinforces the modern design and holds the stems tightly. This

one is heavy pottery with a rough-textured surface. If you choose a light holder put some stones in the bottom for stability. Cut the branches if necessary and arrange them in a massed design to build up to a tree shape. Put some at the back for depth and balance. Force some short-cut lengths of stem inside the container at surface level to make the arrangement firm.

I have covered the surface with oak moss to complete it. You could use moss, bark chips or coconut fibre from a garden centre.

The parcels beneath are all kept in the theme of the Pacific and in neutral colours. They are woven raffia and Pandanus leaf boxes. Some are tied with natural hat trimming, some with classy black satin ribbon. Trimmings are fresh pittosporum berries and lancewood spikes.

*A*n Advent tree gives you a chance to give, and receive, presents for each and every day of the Christmas season. It's an exciting variation of those glittered cardboard Advent calendars from our childhood. An Advent tree is a charming decoration and a fun way to count down to Christmas – especially for young children eagerly awaiting Santa's arrival. It also makes a unique gift.

Advent is the period immediately before the festival of the Nativity, including four Sundays. The number of days will depend on when the Sundays fall. In Germany many families have an Advent wreath, adorned with small images and with four candles, one of which is burnt on each of the four Sundays of Advent. Candles are used too in the Swedish Advent festival on St Lucia's Day, 13 December.

You can use a cut tree or branches from your garden, but as this has to last from 1 December, it's best to buy a small living tree (pictured is Araucaria heterophylla, *the Norfolk pine). Place it in a container to hide its pot, with a saucer underneath to catch water overflow. Choose a little gift, either for each day of Advent or, like the children's calendars, for the first 24 days of December. I used marzipan shapes, hard candy and* trinkets. Buy wide ribbon (about 7 cm) in one or two colours (grosgrain and satin are ideal). Choose any colour combination you like but make sure it will suit your room or the container holding the tree. Cut the ribbon into 25 cm lengths, fold each in half, then stitch or staple into a bag. Trim the tops with pinking shears. Place a gift in each bag. Write numbers on tiny cards or labels, then punch a hole in the corner of each card. Choose a contrasting or matching tie or cord and thread a length through the hole to tie the top of each bag. Either hang the presents from the cord to the tree or tuck them safely between the branches.*

THE PERFECT ROAST TURKEY

Stuff the neck end of the turkey loosely with Lemon Thyme Stuffing, or your favourite stuffing. Close the cavity with poultry skewers using proper string (ie not plastic). Tie the legs together and secure the wings under the body. Weigh the turkey after stuffing and calculate the cooking time (see Cooking Timetable) to have it cooked 30 minutes before you want to carve it. This allows the meat to rest and firm up, making carving easier. Place the turkey breast side up in a roasting dish and brush with 100 g extra melted butter. Cover loosely with tinfoil and cook in a preheated 190°C oven. Fold the tinfoil back 1 hour before the end of the cooking time to brown and crisp the skin. Baste regularly, and test for doneness towards the end of the calculated time. Sometimes a turkey timer is inserted in the bird when you buy it. Otherwise, insert a knife tip or skewer into the thigh. If the juices run clear the turkey is properly cooked through. Removing the wishbone will make carving much easier. Cut off the legs, then slice downwards, working in towards the breast bone.

COOKING TIMETABLE

Oven-ready Weight	Approx Thawing Time in Fridge	Cooking Time Foil Wrapped	Approx No of Servings
0.5–1.5 kg	4–10 hours	1–1.5 hours	2–3
1.5–2.5 kg	10–15 hours	1.5–2 hours	3–6
2.5–3.5 kg	15–18 hours	2–3 hours	6–10
3.5–5.0 kg	18–20 hours	3–3.5 hours	10–15
5.0–7.0 kg	20–24 hours	3.5–4.5 hours	15–20
7.0–9.0 kg	24–30 hours	4.5–5 hours	20–25

LEMON THYME STUFFING

150 g butter
2 large onions, chopped
6 slices toast-cut white bread (made into breadcrumbs in the food processor)
2 tablespoon chopped fresh thyme (or 1 teaspoon dried)
grated rind and juice of 1 lemon
1 cup seedless raisins

Melt the butter in a large bowl in the microwave. Add the chopped onion and cook for 3 minutes. Add the other ingredients and mix well, getting the breadcrumbs well coated in butter.

Tips: Have the stuffing at room temperature and stuff the turkey just before cooking. The stuffing can also be cooked in greased muffin tins, which takes 25–30 minutes and makes it easy to serve. I recommend stuffing the neck end only. Fully stuffing the bird increases the cooking time considerably and by the time the stuffing is cooked right through the meat is dried out. It's much better to cook any extra stuffing as a side dish. The stuffing can be made in advance and stored separately in the fridge.

BABY SAUSAGES WRAPPED IN BACON

Twist and snip some chipolata sausages in half. Wrap each half in a rasher of streaky bacon, securing the bacon with toothpicks. Pop these in around the roasting turkey during the last 30 minutes or so of cooking. Turn a couple of times to crisp the bacon evenly.

CRISPY ROAST POTATOES

Peel even-sized small to medium potatoes and cook in boiling salted water for 5 minutes. Cool. When the potatoes are cold enough to handle, scrape a fork over the sides to rough up the surface. Return to the turkey roasting dish for the last hour of cooking. Turn frequently in the pan drippings for even, crispy roasting.

CRANBERRY ORANGE SAUCE

**juice and grated rind of one
   orange
4 cups fresh or frozen cranberries
2 cups caster sugar
2 cups red wine
1½ cups fresh orange juice**

Place all ingredients (including both orange juices) into a medium-sized saucepan and bring to the boil. Simmer, stirring occasionally, for 30 minutes. Remove and put aside half of the cranberry mixture. Blend the rest in the sauce until smooth. Return to the saucepan with the reserved berries. This sauce can be served warm or cold, and keeps in the fridge for 3–4 weeks.

CHRISTMAS MINCE PIES

MAKES 36 MINI PIES

MINCEMEAT
1 cup raisins, chopped
1/2 cup currants
1/2 cup dates, stones removed and chopped
1/2 cup prunes, stones removed and chopped
150 g crystallised mixed peel
1 teaspoon mixed spice
1/4 cup brown sugar
1/2 cup brandy or sherry
1/2 teaspoon grated lemon rind
1/4 cup lemon juice
1 apple, peeled, cored and grated

Place all ingredients in a saucepan. Bring to the boil and simmer uncovered for 5–10 minutes until the liquid has evaporated. Cool, then store indefinitely in a sealed container in the fridge.

PASTRY
1 1/2 cups flour
1/4 cup custard powder
1/4 cup icing sugar
125 g butter, cut into small cubes
1 egg yolk
2–3 tablespoons cold water

In a food processor, process the flour, custard powder, icing sugar and butter until crumbly. Add the egg yolk and enough cold water to make the ingredients cling together in a ball. Knead the dough on a floured surface until smooth, then cover it in a bowl with plastic clingfilm and refrigerate for 30 minutes. Well grease or spray 3 sets of mini muffin trays. Roll out the pastry to 3 mm thick and press out circles with a 4–5 cm cookie cutter. Press into the prepared tins. Fill each with a heaped teaspoon of Christmas mincemeat. Cut out little pastry lids to cover the muffin cups and press them down to seal. Bake at 180°C for 15–20 minutes until pale golden and crisp. Cool in the tin, then twist around to loosen the bases and carefully remove the pies. Dust them with icing sugar if you like.

VARIATIONS
Star topped mince pies
Instead of placing pastry lids on top of the mincemeat, cut out pastry star shapes with a tiny cookie cutter and place these on top. Cook as above, but the baking time may be quicker, say 12–15 minutes.

Open mince pies
Line the muffin tins with pastry as above, then insert a little screwed-up ball of tinfoil into each muffin cup. Cook without the mincemeat at 180°C for 12–15 minutes until golden and pale. Remove the foil ball carefully and cook a further 3 minutes. This is a simple version of baking blind. Pile a heaped teaspoonful of mincemeat into each case. These do not need further cooking.

Lattice-topped pies
Roll out the pastry to 3 mm and cut it into long strips. Weave a lattice pattern with the strips, then cut out 3–4 cm rounds of this lattice to fit the muffin cups. Press gently on top and proceed as for lidded muffins.

Tips: In an airtight container these will keep for up to 2 weeks. Mince pies freeze extremely well, and empty pastry cases keep well in an airtight container or frozen.

CHOCOLATE CRANBERRY PORT TRUFFLES

MAKES 50–60 GOOD-SIZED TRUFFLES

150 g butter
375 g (1 packet) dark chocolate melts
2 cups craisins (dried cranberries)
½ cup port
3 cups icing sugar

TO DIP AND GARNISH
750 g (2 packets) dark chocolate melts
375 g (1 packet) white chocolate melts
10 glacé cherries (red and green)

Place the butter and chocolate melts in a microwave-safe bowl and cook on medium until melted (about 4 minutes), stirring several times (see page 26 for tips on melting chocolate). Put the craisins and port in a small microwave-safe bowl and cook on high for 1–2 minutes until the craisins plump up. Combine both mixtures with the icing sugar and chill until firm enough to roll into large marble-sized truffles. Place the truffles on a tinfoil-covered tray and freeze until really solid (about 2 hours). (At this stage they can be stored in a plastic container in the freezer for months.) Before you want to eat the truffles, melt two packets of dark chocolate melts in the microwave on medium power, stirring often. Dip the frozen (or at least well-chilled) truffles in the melted chocolate, using a chocolate dipping fork. Allow them to set on a tinfoil-lined tray. Melt the white chocolate and drip it down the sides to look like custard on top of a pudding. Top each one with cut pieces of red and green cherry so they look like miniature Christmas puddings. Store in a cool place but not in the fridge or freezer or the chocolate will weep.

TRADITIONAL RICH CHRISTMAS CAKE
WITH TOFFEED FRUIT AND NUT GLAZE

1.5 kg mixed dried fruit	500 g butter, softened
250 g glacé cherries, red and green	1½ cups brown sugar
100 g mixed peel	8 eggs
1 tablespoon grated orange rind	2 bananas, mashed
1 tablespoon grated lemon rind	1 teaspoon vanilla
2 tablespoons lemon juice	4 cups flour
½ cup brandy	1 cup self-raising flour

Place the mixed dried fruit, cherries, mixed peel, orange rind, lemon rind, lemon juice and brandy in a large bowl. Mix well and leave overnight. In a separate bowl, cream the butter and sugar until it is light and fluffy. Add the eggs one at a time, beating well after each addition, then add the bananas and vanilla. Thoroughly stir in the fruit mixture and add the flours. Mix until well combined. Place in a deep 25 cm cake tin, which has been lined with two thicknesses of brown paper and one thickness of greaseproof paper. Bake in a slow oven (150°C) for about 3½ hours, or until a skewer inserted into the middle of the cake comes out clean.

TOFFEED FRUIT AND NUT GLAZE

1 cup sugar
½ cup cold water
1 cup (approx) red glacé cherries
1 cup (approx) green glacé cherries
2 cups mixed nuts (brazil, almond, pecan, walnut, hazelnut)

Place the sugar and water in a small saucepan over a gentle heat. Swirl the saucepan around until the sugar is dissolved, then slowly bring to the boil. Boil (not too vigorously) without stirring until the sugar caramelises to a light golden colour (10–15 minutes). Remove from the heat and cool slightly. Arrange the cherries and nuts over the top of the cake and very carefully drizzle the toffee over the surface, letting it drip down the sides. Do be careful as sugar burns are very nasty. Allow the toffee to set, then transfer the cake to a serving plate or cake stand. If you keep the cake covered and in a cool place, the toffee will stay crisp for days. (You just have to watch out for sneaky folk nibbling bits off.)

> **Tip:** This cake looks quite spectacular but is rather a challenge to cut into neat portions. I usually go for a slice of cake with a 'chopped' piece of toffee topping.

*T*op left is a traditional round fir wreath

trimmed with cones, gold pears and

ribbon. This can be adapted into a long

hanging wreath (top right) or by using

different materials can be given a more

modern, southern hemisphere look

(bottom left).

TOP LEFT: Take a round artificial fir wreath base and on the back at its top loop on floristry wire with which to hang the wreath. This will help you get the balance right while you are putting it together. Keep the wire short so it does not show above the top of the wreath. (Alternatively, if you want to have a ribbon holding the wreath, tie it on now. A good idea is to use wire or string and then wind the ribbon on top as a decorative extra. Here I have chosen to use ribbon just as a decoration.)

Take some dried cones and hook a piece of wire over some of the cone 'petals' at the base. Twist the wire in a tight spiral to make an artificial stem. Fasten these in groups around the stems of the fir. A hot glue gun is useful for the pears (and in fact to fasten everything onto this wreath). Or you can use PVA. Glue the centre of a piece of wire onto the bottom of each pear and bend both ends downwards to make a false double stem. Fasten these onto the fir.

Make a bow by looping one or two types of ribbon and leaving the right number of tails to correspond with the loops. Tightly bend some wire around the centre and twist a couple of times. Secure this directly in line with the wire on which the wreath will hang, but this time at the front and not the back. Wire-edged ribbon sits well and stays in place. This wreath would also look lovely with just natural cones and no metallic fruit or ribbon.

TOP RIGHT: This large wreath is made by cutting a long artificial fir mantelpiece garland into three pieces. Cut one piece a little longer for the centre branch. Wire or tie them securely together at the top. Manipulate the wired fir stems so that the whole unit has quite a flat back. Now make a hanging loop with wire or string at the centre top. Choose some large cones for the centre top, or you could use a huge cluster of smaller cones. Wire them as described for the round fir wreath. Attach them at intervals, keeping the smaller cones for lower down the branches for balance. Buy single artificial fruit, or, as I have done here, branches of artificial plums that I have cut from their main stem, leaving a few leaves and a little stem. Twist some wire around these and attach at intervals. Alternatively you could use all the fruit at the top. Attach the ribbon in the same way as described for the round fir wreath caption and nestle it in among the top cones.

BOTTOM LEFT: Choose a type of eucalyptus or other foliage that has supple stems and abundant foliage in good condition. Pick plenty. Floristry wire is best here, but you could use string. Begin by gathering a few stems into a straight bunch and wiring them together once, quite near the top. Take another few stems of a similar volume and place them on top, a little further down the length of the first bunch. Wire these around again – this time the wire will go around both bunches of stems. Keep the wire out of sight. Continue until you have a long sausage of bound leaves to the length that will give you a circle the size of your choice.

If some of the stems are too woody and inflexible cut them, but be careful not to cut too many woody stems out as these help to keep the wreath stable. Allow lots of the leaves to remain free to give a generous appearance. Bend the sausage into a circle and secure underneath. This wreath looks lovely fresh but in our summer Christmas climate be prepared for it to dry quickly. You can see here how lovely it looks dried.

Make a wire loop at the back to hang it from. If you want to add decorations, use something natural such as shells or cones. I have used paua shells and their blue-green hues look great with the grey-green gum leaves. Paua have tiny holes that are perfect for putting wire or string through to attach them to the stems of the wreath at even intervals. This wreath doesn't need a ribbon. Keep it natural.

Christmas wreaths do not have to go on the wall. The artificial wreaths used here have a wire base that makes each a portable container once it is arranged. These are available from a Christmas supply shop. If you can't find one, use a bottomless one and arrange it in situ or place it on a complementary tray or platter.

LEFT: A raised wooden stand (this is an Indonesian ceremonial table called a dulang) gives grandeur, while allowing for things like platters of food to be placed underneath it. You could also arrange the wreath on the table top or on a tray. A large triple-wicked candle is set in the centre. Mixed dried cones are placed in groups for the larger ones and singly for the stems of larch cones. To add a metallic touch of Christmas I have included artificial gold walnuts and gold and cream ribbons. This looks super and takes only a couple of minutes.

OPPOSITE PAGE: This wreath has a taste of the sea. Fill the centre with items that whisper of the waves – shells, seaweed, sponges or stones. Pop some shells among the fir twigs around the outside too.

RIGHT: The table wreath here has had a six-candle holder placed inside it. It's one of my favourite candle-holders (see page 184 where it is shown undecorated in my store cupboard) – it looks unassuming and it's so versatile. Fresh green grapes fill the centre and six fresh green pears are placed at even intervals around the bottom edge. Three flourishes of lime green ribbon add a festive touch for a midsummer Christmas. If you're busting for bright colours, blaze a trail with red apples, red chillies, red ribbon and red candles.

If you're going away right on Christmas and don't want the full-on hassle of a tree with all the trimmings – or if you're stuck for space – try this simple biscuit branch. You could also have a whole tree made in the same way as the teddy bear tree on page 164. I have tied Jo's Christmas tree biscuits to a chunky lichen-covered branch using fine multi-coloured cord threaded through the hole in the biscuit.

To add substance, I've tied a ribbon (picking out the colours from the cord) on the branch just above the biscuit to look as if it is also threaded through the tasty Yuletide morsel.

GINGERBREAD COOKIE DOUGH

MAKES 48 COOKIES

250 g butter, softened
1 cup icing sugar
1 egg
1/2 cup unsulphured molasses
4 cups flour

1 tablespoon cocoa
1 tablespoon ground ginger
2 teaspoons mixed spice
1 teaspoon baking soda
1/2 teaspoon salt

In a large bowl using an electric beater mix the butter and icing sugar until light and fluffy. Add the egg, then the molasses, and mix well. Add the rest of the ingredients and mix all together thoroughly on a low speed. Divide the dough into 4 pieces and flatten into discs. Wrap in plastic clingfilm and refrigerate until firm – at least 2 hours. (If you like, the dough can be frozen at this stage.) On a lightly floured surface roll the dough to 5 mm thickness and cut with cookie cutters. Transfer to a baking-paper-lined baking tray and make a hole in each cookie to thread string or ribbon through if you want to hang them on your Christmas tree. A meat skewer or bamboo toothpick is perfect for the job. Bake at 180°C for 10–15 minutes. The cookies should be just colouring brown at the edges. Cool for 5 minutes on the oven tray and remove them to a wire rack. Store in an airtight container when completely cold.

ROYAL ICING

2 egg whites
2 tablespoons water
1 tablespoon strained lemon juice

2 1/2 cups icing sugar
food colouring (optional)

Place all ingredients in a large bowl, beat with electric mixer until fluffy, thick and shiny. (Add more icing sugar if required.) Pipe decorative features onto the cookies. The icing can also be refrigerated for several days but may need to be re-beaten to return it to a workable consistency.

LEFT: *Nothing could be simpler than a battered old lead plate, set with three chunky, dribbling beeswax candles and a sprig of holly. The minimal wire tree is decorated with tiny pewter bells, creating a frugal setting with lots of charm. There is even a spiritual feel to the scene, with two family Bibles reflecting the religious significance of Christmas.*

BELOW: *This simple object in itself engenders thoughts of Christmas. The crude Mexican tin wall sconce needs only a sprig of cedar and a lit beeswax candle to evoke Christmas night.*

OPPOSITE PAGE: *This simple decoration makes an understated design for a mantelpiece. A bought topiary-style Christmas tree made of dried leaves that have been bound onto a frame is the starting point. The tree is flat backed and has an attached flat wooden base so it sits neatly against the wall. Huge beeswax and paraffin pillar candles are randomly placed beside the tree, tapering down to lower heights on the outside edge for balance. Dried moss adds a simple touch at the base.*

OLD-FASHIONED ROUND CHRISTMAS PUDDING

SERVES 8–10

3½ cups seedless raisins
1¼ cups sultanas
1¼ cups currants
1 cup glacé cherries, chopped
150 g crystallised peel
1 cup blanched almonds, chopped
6 slices white toast-cut bread
  made into fresh breadcrumbs
250 g suet (beef or vegetable),
  grated or shredded
1 teaspoon cinnamon
½ teaspoon grated nutmeg
6 eggs
½ cup beer or Guinness
¼ cup brandy
1 teaspoon molasses

In a large bowl mix the dried fruit, peel, almonds, breadcrumbs, suet and spices. In another bowl whisk together the eggs, beer, brandy and molasses. Stir through the fruit mixture. Cover and leave for a time – preferably overnight. Well grease a pudding basin or mould and spoon the mixture in. Secure the lid or cover the basin with buttered baking paper then tinfoil, tied over with string. Put the basin on a rack or upturned saucer inside a large saucepan. Pour in enough boiling water to come three-quarters of the way up the basin. Cover the saucepan and steam for 6–7 hours (4–5 hours for smaller puddings), adding extra water as needed. Remove the pudding, take off its cover and leave to cool. Then cover it in clean baking paper and foil and store, either in the fridge or a cool dark pantry. To serve, steam the pudding for 1 hour or microwave to heat through. Serve with Brandy Butter, cream or custard.

TO FLAME CHRISTMAS PUDDING

Warm a quarter of a glass of brandy in a tiny saucepan or, easier still, in the microwave – bring it to the temperature of drinkable tea or coffee. Place the Christmas pudding on a platter with sides to prevent spillages. Pour the warm brandy over and carefully ignite with a match. Be careful not to slosh the brandy around – shoes on fire is not a good festive look – and don't forget to turn the lights down low for full effect.

BRANDY BUTTER

200 g butter, softened
4 cups icing sugar
½ cup brandy

Whip all ingredients together until smooth and fluffy. Serve at room temperature with hot steamed Christmas pudding. The mixture will harden when it is kept in the fridge and may need to be re-whipped and warmed to soften it again.

RIGHT: *A home-made Christmas pudding makes a wonderful gift. And to make it even more special, buy an inexpensive pudding bowl to make it in and give this as part of the gift. I have found some lovely old pudding bowls in junk shops. They remind me of my mother and her lovely Christmas puds made in the copper in our wash-house when I was a child.*

Inexpensive cotton gingham fabric makes a novel wrapping. Try a colour scheme like this smart black and white instead of the traditional red and green. Cut the gingham into a large square to make an even shape for wrapping. Gather it up in the centre and tie with a piece of string. Then add a gorgeous ribbon, a mini bottle of brandy for pouring over the pud, and a cluster of berries to complete a scrumptious gift.

BIRTHDAYS

Why not choose a theme for a birthday party? It's so much fun and creates a great atmosphere.

Beautiful flowers and a restrained colour palette are lovely for a female birthday and how about a fishing theme for a man? We've also included an Irish theme for a man with connections to the Emerald Isle or simply a love for Guinness, whiskey or just plain blarney! For a child's curiosity and delight, go for bright, uninhibited primary colours.

We've carried the themes right through into choice of plates and napkins. For the Irish birthday party, for example, we've chosen rustic dishes, pots and cutlery to complement the homely food. The Hummingbird Cake is served on a classy silver tray to bring out the elegance of the flowers and the cake.

Ensure those parties aren't something to be dreaded with these quick and easy recipes.

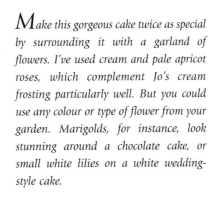

Make this gorgeous cake twice as special by surrounding it with a garland of flowers. I've used cream and pale apricot roses, which complement Jo's cream frosting particularly well. But you could use any colour or type of flower from your garden. Marigolds, for instance, look stunning around a chocolate cake, or small white lilies on a white wedding-style cake.

Use a low-edged tray so the garland is not hidden. I placed a round ring of wet floral foam straight onto a silver tray, about 5 cm in from the outside edge. If you can't get a ring of foam, cut blocks of foam to fit. If you put the inverted cake tin in the centre you can stand the cake on it so that it can be seen and not lost in the flowers. It's essential to keep the cake away from the wet foam so as to avoid any sticky messes. I used a round

chopping board to raise the cake as this also provided a good chopping surface for cutting it. What the eye can't see . . .

Begin the arrangement with trails of fine ivy with supple stems. Long trails are easier to secure in place. Spike the cut end of the ivy into the foam on the outside edge and anchor it at intervals with small hairpins of florist's wire. This is a wonderful 'secret weapon' to have in the cupboard. If you can't get florist's wire

you could use real hairpins. Use several pieces of ivy, then add some short rose leaves. Lastly cut the roses short and spike them in groups of three at intervals around the ring. (They will last longer if you've conditioned them by giving them a long drink of water for a day before.) A few rosehips and unopened buds gave this a natural garden touch.

Put the cake in place last. See – you really can have your cake and eat it!

HUMMINGBIRD CAKE

225 g can crushed pineapple,
undrained
3 bananas, mashed
1 cup chopped blanched almonds
2 teaspoons vanilla essence
1½ cups oil

3 eggs
3 cups flour
1 teaspoon baking soda
1 teaspoon ground ginger
1 cup sugar
½ teaspoon salt

Preheat the oven to 180°C. Grease and line a 23 cm cake tin with baking paper. Mix all ingredients in a food processor until just combined. Pour into the prepared tin and bake 1½ hours until golden brown. Leave in tin for 15 minutes, then turn out and cool completely on a wire rack.

FROSTING
50 g butter, softened
250 g cream cheese, softened

1 teaspoon vanilla
2 cups icing sugar

Beat the butter and cream cheese together until smooth. Beat in the vanilla and icing sugar. Split the cake into 2 or 3 layers, fill with frosting, and spread it over the top and down the sides as well. Leave it to set before cutting.

WHITE CHOCOLATE AND CANDIED PEEL TRUFFLES

MAKES 40

100 g butter
2 packets (375 g each) white chocolate melts
2 cups icing sugar
150 g mixed crystallised peel
2 tablespoons orange liqueur (Cointreau or Grand Marnier) or use fresh orange juice

Melt the butter and 1 packet of the chocolate melts together in the microwave or over a saucepan of hot water (see tip on page 26). Stir in the icing sugar, citrus peel and orange liqueur and form into small balls. (If the mixture is too soft, chill for 20 minutes, then roll into balls.) Chill the balls for at least 1 hour in the fridge, or store them indefinitely in a covered container in the freezer for dipping later.

TO DIP TRUFFLES

Melt the second packet of white chocolate melts, following the instructions on the packet. Dip the chilled (or frozen) truffles in the melted chocolate, using a chocolate dipping fork made especially for this job. Drip off any excess chocolate and allow the truffles to set on a tinfoil-covered tray. Keep the finished truffles in a cool place but not in the fridge as the chocolate tends to sweat.

PREVIOUS PAGE: *I've kept this birthday table setting in the soft colours of cream, off-white, coffee and a touch of gold. The Charlotte Russe-shaped containers brimming with narcissus are for a special dinner. Off-white napkins are tied with gold organza ribbon and trimmed with pressed ginkgo leaves that have been given a light dusting of bronze floral spray. (The leaves could have the guests' names printed on them.) A menu with the initial of the birthday girl is popped inside the top of the napkin. Rose-shaped candles are set on bought natural skeletonised leaves – pressed ginkgo leaves would be good for this too. They are placed randomly over the table top.*

I have imitated the classic dessert Charlotte Russe (a round mould of Bavarian cream lined with sponge fingers) for the container for this table setting. Buy sponge fingers from the supermarket and rummage in your cupboards for inexpensive plastic bowls. (You could even use an ice-cream container.) If necessary cut the top lip off the bowl. This makes it easier for the flowers to come right up to the outside edge. Use a hot-glue gun (or other suitable glue such as PVA) to secure the sponge fingers neatly upright around the outside of the plastic bowl. I trimmed the container with a crushed ribbon, which sat more neatly on the surface than a flat

ribbon. Crumple a small piece of 5 cm-mesh chicken wire and place it inside the bowl. (Wire is easier to use for soft stems like narcissus, which can bend when put in wet floral foam.) Add water (being careful to avoid drops on the sponge fingers) and begin arranging massed narcissus in the bowl. Bought narcissus bunches never have leaves included so try and find some narcissus or similar spiky leaves from the garden. They make the whole arrangement look garden-picked.

*H*ere's a birthday spread for the man in your life. A hundred (yes, I counted them!) red anemones make a bold statement arranged in an antique wooden pig trough (a long bread basket would do fine). This massed effect appears extravagant but is easy to achieve. I have put several blocks of wet floral foam inside the trough. The anemones are cut quite short and spiked into the foam all at almost the same low level. A few sprigs of red nandina berries (you could use rose-hips) add another texture and green moss fills in the gaps. The novel red lilies in the old papier-mâché pots are amaryllis. Their bases are trimmed with moss to hide the plastic pot that sits inside. The dinnerware is coarse Spanish and Portuguese pottery, maintaining the rustic theme.

BEEF AND GUINNESS CASSEROLE

SERVES 6–8

¼ cup olive oil
6 rashers bacon, chopped
3 large onions, peeled and
 roughly chopped
6–8 cloves garlic (2 teaspoons
 crushed)
1.5 kg beef steak, cut into cubes
 or chunky pieces
2 tablespoons flour
2 cups Guinness (or beer)

2 cups beef stock
½ teaspoon dried thyme
3 carrots, peeled and thickly sliced
500 g button mushrooms
12–16 small pickling onions,
 peeled and left whole
salt and freshly ground black
 pepper
tablespoon chopped parsley

Preheat the oven to 150°C. Heat the olive oil in a large ovenproof pan or casserole on the stove top, add the chopped bacon and sizzle for 4–5 minutes. Add the onion and crushed garlic and cook a further 2 minutes. Dust the cubes of beef with the flour and add them to the pan. Stir-fry for 3–4 minutes, then add the Guinness, stock, thyme, carrots, mushrooms and baby onions. Season generously with salt and freshly ground black pepper. Stir, then cover the casserole and bake for half an hour or so. Remove the lid and check the seasoning. If desired add a little Worcestershire sauce. Cook uncovered for a further 30–45 minutes. Garnish with a sprinkle of chopped parsley.

> **Tips:** Serve with Colcannon, or mashed plain or baked potatoes. This casserole improves upon reheating. Onions just need to be tossed with olive oil and a sprinkle of salt and roasted in a hot oven (200°C) for 35–40 minutes. Stir a couple of times during cooking.

SIMPLE ROAST ONIONS

1 medium onion per person
oil

Slice onions from top to bottom through the roots. Leave the papery onion skins intact. Place cut side down in a well-oiled roasting dish or baking tray. Cook in a hot oven, 200°C, for approximately 35–40 minutes until golden brown and cooked though.

COLCANNON

SERVES 4

6 medium potatoes, peeled and
** cubed**
1 onion, finely chopped
3 cups (approx) sliced cabbage
1 leek, finely sliced
50 g butter (or to taste)
½ cup milk
3 tablespoons chopped parsley
salt and lots of freshly ground
** black pepper**

Boil the potatoes in salted water until soft. When they are cooked add the onion, cabbage and leek to the water and simmer 2–3 minutes, until they are softened. Drain in a colander. To the same saucepan add the butter and milk. Stir until butter has melted. Return the vegetables to the saucepan with the parsley. Mash with a potato masher, adding extra butter (or margarine) and salt and pepper to taste.

DRAMBUIE, BLUE CHEESE AND WALNUT SPREAD

150 g blue cheese, crumbled
150 g cream cheese
¼ cup Drambuie
½ cup chopped walnuts

Mix the blue cheese, cream cheese and Drambuie together until smoothly combined. Stir the chopped walnuts through, adding a little milk if the mixture is too stiff. Spread on Garlic Pita Crisps (page 133) or crackers.

IRISH SODA BREAD

4 cups flour
1 teaspoon baking soda
1 teaspoon salt
50 g butter, melted
2 cups buttermilk (or milk)

Preheat the oven to 180°C. Mix all the ingredients together in a food processor. Turn out onto a floured surface. Shape the dough into a 18–20 cm round cob and place on a well-greased oven tray. Score the top surface in a criss-cross pattern with a knife and dust with extra flour. Bake for 40 minutes. The base should sound hollow when tapped. Best served warm.

INDIVIDUAL DEEP
APPLE PIES

MAKES 4

2½ cups flour
200 g butter
6 tablespoons sugar

4 egg yolks
2 x 800 g cans apples slices or
6 cups cooked apples slices

Preheat the oven to 170°C. Place all the ingredients except apple in a food processor. Run the machine until the pastry clumps together around the blade. Divide the pastry mixture into 5 portions. Press out 4 of these to line the base and sides of 4 individual spring-form tins (7 x 4 x approx 2 cm deep). Fill with the apple filling. Crumble the remaining portion of pastry over the top of the little pies. Bake for 40–45 minutes until lightly golden and crispy. Cool in the tins. Carefully remove the sides of the tins and slide the pies off base onto a serving plate. Dust with icing sugar and serve warm with cream or ice-cream.

A birthday drinks party for a keen fisherman. A cane fishing creel is an unusual floral container but evokes the seafood theme of this party. (You could use a picnic hamper or any small basket.) Put a watertight container inside the basket and use either wet floral foam or crushed 5 cm chicken wire with water. Use only mixed foliages – you don't need flowers to make a fantastic arrangement. Here I've chosen camellia branches, green berries and some stems of authentic-looking artificial grasses and succulents. You'll have to forgive the artistic licence used to include pheasant and turkey feathers in two groups among the foliage, and the lovely old duck decoy and bought feather-covered eggs at the base.

131

TINY BREAD CASES

1 loaf sandwich-cut brown or white bread (or a mixture)

Preheat the oven to 180°C. Using a round cookie cutter 3–4 cm in diameter cut out two rounds from each slice of bread. Carefully press the bread rounds into deep mini muffin trays and spray with oil. Place a second tray on top (to keep the bread case shape) and bake for 10–15 minutes, until crisp and golden. Cool on a wire rack and store in an airtight container until required.

SUGGESTED FILLINGS
- Cream cheese with smoked oysters, garnished with a sprig of dill.
- Pan-fried button mushrooms with créme fraîche and fresh sage.
- Pesto topped with cherry tomatoes.
- Prawns and tomato with mayonnaise.
- Baby scallops marinated in lime juice with coconut cream.
- Smoked salmon and cream cheese topped with caviar.

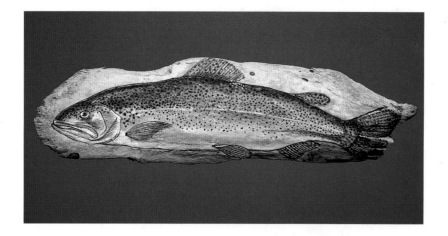

GARLIC PITA CRISPS

pita bread
olive oil
garlic salt

Preheat the oven to 180°C. Using scissors cut the pita bread into triangles and split them open. Drizzle generously with olive oil and sprinkle with garlic salt. Bake for 10–12 minutes until crisp and golden. Cool on a wire rack and store in an airtight container. These can be used as dippers or as bases with sour cream, smoked salmon, smoked salmon roe and garnished with a spring of dill.

ANCHOVY FINGERS

1 small can (approx 100 g) anchovies in oil
2 sheets frozen puff pastry, thawed
egg wash (1 tablespoon water mixed with an egg yolk)
1–2 teaspoons fennel seeds (or substitute sesame seeds)

Preheat the oven to 200°C. Drain the anchovies and roughly chop them. Brush a sheet of pastry with water, then spread with the chopped anchovies – as if you are buttering a piece of toast. Lay the second sheet of pastry over the top. Roll with a rolling pin to really stick the sheets together and spread the pastry to about 3 mm thick. Brush with the egg wash and sprinkle with the fennel or sesame seeds. Cut into strips the size of your finger and lay these on a baking tray. Cook for 15–20 minutes until puffed and golden. Serve warm or store in an airtight container (see right of photograph on page 131).

Tip: These freeze well for reheating in the oven later.

Simple hand-crafted boxes like this Shaker box and the old crudely made collar box make wonderful gifts that don't need to be wrapped. They can also be enhanced by using simple but novel trimmings. Here I have used an interesting trim on the Shaker box – coarse hemp webbing. The small parcel is tied with hat banding and the fine trim on the hand-made paper-wrapped box is seagrass. The star card was made by a dear friend, and the charming hand-shaped card is the traditional Shaker symbol meaning 'Hands to work, hearts to God.' I wired together cones, gum nuts and wheat to form a posy redolent of the woods, edged with dried leaves. A feather makes an interesting trim on the hand-made paper parcel.

RIGHT: *A gift for a boatie. The fudge (see page 136) is put into a mesh bag, tied with leather boat laces (in keeping with our boating theme) and placed inside this charming old wooden toy boat.*

Born to Read   Paul Verdon

PAUL VERDON   THE POWER BEHIND THE ALL

RUSSIAN FUDGE

MAKES 36 PIECES

3½ cups sugar
125 g butter
3 tablespoons golden syrup
½ cup milk
½ teaspoon salt
200 g sweetened condensed milk (half the standard 400 g can)
2 teaspoons vanilla essence

Place all ingredients except the vanilla into a medium-heavy saucepan. Warm over a gentle heat until the sugar has dissolved. Bring to a gentle boil and cook for 15–20 minutes, until it reaches the soft-ball stage (120°C). Remove from the heat and add the vanilla. Beat (I use an electric mixer) until the fudge is creamy and thick and has lost its gloss. Pour into a greased 20 cm cake pan. Score the top and break into pieces when cold.

IRISH WHISKEY CREAM LIQUEUR

4 egg yolks
400 g can sweetened condensed milk
300 ml cream
3 tablespoons chocolate dessert topping or sauce
2 teaspoons coconut essence
450 ml whiskey

Beat the egg yolks until thick and pale. Add the other ingredients and beat until thick. Pour into clean bottles and store in the fridge for up to 10 days.

For children's birthdays go for bold and bright. Don't worry about clashing colours. I kept to red, yellow and white for impact but the sky's the limit: you could choose your child's favourite colours or let them do the selecting.

MOIST CHOCOLATE BIRTHDAY CAKE

SERVES 10–12

2 cups caster sugar	**2 tablespoons malt vinegar**
3 cups self-raising flour	**2 tablespoons golden syrup**
2 teaspoons baking soda	**2 teaspoons vanilla**
1/2 cup cocoa	**1 1/2 cups cooking oil**
4 eggs	**1 egg**
2 cups milk	

Preheat the oven to 180°C. Combine all the dry ingredients and put aside. Separate 3 eggs (the other one is used whole). In a large bowl beat the 3 egg whites until stiff. Set aside. Combine the milk and vinegar, then add the golden syrup, whole egg, egg yolks, vanilla and oil. Beat well. Mix the wet and dry ingredients together, then gently fold in the beaten egg whites. Divide the mixture between 2 well-greased or baking-paper-lined 23–25 cm cake tins. Bake for 25–30 minutes. Cool completely on a wire rack. Spread one cake with White Fluffy Frosting, place the other cake on top and spread the top and sides with the remaining frosting.

WHITE FLUFFY FROSTING

2 egg whites
2 tablespoons water
2 1/2–3 cups icing sugar

Place all ingredients in a large bowl and beat with an electric mixer until fluffy, thick and shiny. This icing can be refrigerated for several days but may need to be beaten to return it to a workable consistency.

Tips: Based on Soonafai's Chocolate Cake from the Chelsea *Sugar and Spice* collection, this is easy to make and big enough for a large birthday celebration. The flag layer cake in the picture took 2 batches of mixture. The second batch was divided between 4 smaller tins and layered up accordingly. All layers were then frosted, requiring 1 1/2 batches of frosting.

Jo's white-frosted flag layer cake uses the Moist Chocolate Birthday Cake recipe, which provided a clean palette for me to decorate for a child. I bought 4 cm-wide wire-edged ribbon (so that the flags would 'fly') in three patterns. Each flag is 8 cm long, cut with an inward 'V' shape at one end. I use wooden satay sticks for these – toothpicks are too short. Run a narrow strip of glue down the edge of the straight end of the ribbon. Roll this around the stick for about 1 cm, leaving a tiny piece of the stick showing at the top. I made 30 flags for this cake (allow yourself plenty of time!). Buy sweets in your chosen colours to decorate the edges of the cake and to define the levels. Cut the satay sticks to a suitable length and spike them in so that the flags fly in different directions. I found the tall fine candles at a Chinese food and accessory shop.

CHEESE AND PINEAPPLE SAVOURIES

MAKES 36 BITE-SIZE PORTIONS

3 sheets pre-rolled thawed flaky or puff pastry
2 cups grated cheese
1½ cups of crushed or chopped pineapple (drained)
2 eggs
¾ cup cream
salt and freshly ground black pepper

Preheat the oven to 180°C. Using a 4 cm cookie cutter press out 36 circles of pastry to line 3 trays of mini muffin tins. Sprinkle some cheese into each cup and divide the crushed or chopped drained pineapple between them. Beat the eggs, cream and salt and pepper together and pour into a small jug. Fill each cup half to three-quarters with this filling. Bake for 15–20 minutes until puffed and golden. Twist to loosen and cool on a wire rack. Serve warm. These freeze well for

ABOVE: *Small acetate suitcases provide a tempting holder for party favours to take home. I've kept the contents in the red and yellow theme of the party table and tied them each with two ribbons in matching colours. These make a fun change from the usual party bags.*

*D*ig into the sandpit for some colourful buckets – not too big. These ones are painted metal but plastic beach buckets are fine too. Inside wedge a block of wet floral foam.

Buy some large lollipops and extend their stems by wiring on some satay sticks or chopsticks. This will ensure they rise above the other decorations. Poke one lollipop into the centre of the wet foam in each bucket.

Buy tulle in bright colours – the more garish, the better! Cut small squares of tulle, bunch each at the centre and secure with wire to form a makeshift bow and stem of wire. Using the stem, spike the tulle bows into the foam. Add a few leaves. I've used angelica but you could use camellia, geranium – anything that's in the garden as long as it's not too soft. Add three or five short-cut bright-coloured gerberas to each bucket.

Set the buckets in the centre of the table surrounded by a scattering of lollies . . . and wait for the fights to start over who gets the lollipop! (It might be wise to do one for each of your little guests, as long as you're not into double figures!) You could add bright candles and tiny gifts too.

GUMMY SWEET JELLIES

Make up some brightly coloured jelly according to packet instructions. Leave it to firm up and when it is nearly set, gently push a number of colourful gummy sweets into the jelly. Try dinosaur shapes – and snakes and bears, etc. Refrigerate until set.

Here's a fun children's party table decoration – if it lasts long enough. I bought outsize liquorice allsorts from the supermarket and made holes in them with metal skewers. Then I threaded allsorts and gerbera heads alternately onto wooden satay sticks and finished with a bright bow on each end. As a finishing touch you could put the names of the children on a card tied to each kebab.

MARBLE CUPCAKES

MAKES 12

3 eggs
¾ cup sugar
1 cup flour
1 teaspoon baking powder
50 g butter, melted

2 tablespoons boiling water
1 teaspoon vanilla essence
1 tablespoon cocoa
2–3 drops red or pink food
    colouring

Preheat the oven to 180°C. Beat the eggs until thick, then add the sugar and beat until the mixture is thick, creamy and pale. Fold in the flour and baking powder, then the melted butter, boiling water and vanilla. Divide the mixture into 3 equal quantities in separate bowls. To one part add the cocoa and mix until smooth. To the second bowl add the food colouring and mix until evenly blended. Leave the third mixture plain. Using a dessertspoon, ladle equal parts of each mixture into paper cup cases and stir around a little to swirl the mixtures together. (Don't overmix – you want marble, not uniform brown.) Place the filled cup cases in muffin tins to support them while baking. Bake for 15–20 minutes until well risen. When cooked the cakes will spring back if lightly touched. Cool on a wire rack, then ice and garnish.

ICING

1 tablespoon butter
2 tablespoons boiling water
1–1½ cups icing sugar

2 tablespoons cocoa or
    2 drops pink food colouring

Melt the butter with the water. Add 1 cup icing sugar together with either cocoa or pink food colouring, adding extra icing sugar as needed to make a smooth, spreadable icing. Spread over the top of each cupcake and garnish with sweets or as desired.

LEFT: *To make edible mice, mould chocolate fondant cake icing (available in 500 g packages in the supermarket) into* *mouse shapes. Add almond halves for ears, and narrow red licorice straps for the tails.*

DINOSAUR BISCUITS

MAKES 16

250 g butter, softened
$^3/_4$ cup icing sugar
$^1/_2$ cup cornflour
1$^1/_2$ cups flour

Preheat the oven to 150°C. Beat the butter and icing sugar until creamy. Mix in the cornflour and flour. On a floured surface, roll out the dough to 3 mm thick and press out shapes with a dinosaur cookie cutter. Carefully place on a greased oven tray, or a tray lined with baking paper. Prick with a fork. Bake for 25–30 minutes, until the shortbread is pale but crisp. Cool on a wire rack and store in an airtight container.

ICING

2 egg whites
2 cups icing sugar (approx)
2–3 drops food colouring

Beat the egg whites until frothy, then beat in the icing sugar and food colouring, mixing thoroughly to a thick glossy icing consistency. Spoon into a piping bag fitted with a fine detailing nozzle. Ice some edging and dinosaur details on the biscuits.

Check out your child's toy cupboard, books and magazines for other shapes to use as templates. As long as there are no thin bits that could break off, you can use any shape. Keep it simple and use icing, glacé cherries, sweets or hundreds and thousands for detailing.

ANNIVERSARIES

The older you get, the more anniversaries you have to celebrate, though the prospect of noisy parties is often less appealing.

So we've gone for celebrating anniversaries with stylish high teas, recalling the special days of the past. We've chosen a willow pattern and lemon theme, an old-world lavender and violet look and a golden note for those golden weddings and other events that require nothing but the best.

The meanings of some of the anniversaries may give you decorating, food and presentation ideas.

- First – paper
- Second – cotton
- Third – leather
- Fourth – fruit and flowers
- Fifth – wood
- Sixth – sugar
- Seventh – wool
- Eighth – bronze
- Ninth – pottery
- Tenth – tin
- Twelfth – silk and fine linen

- Fifteenth – crystal
- Twentieth – china
- Twenty-five – silver
- Thirtieth – pearl
- Thirty-fifth – coral
- Forty – ruby
- Forty-fifth – sapphire
- Fifty – gold
- Fifty-five – emerald
- Sixty – diamond
- Seventieth – platinum

The sugar bowl of my mother's willow pattern china set is my container for a pretty spring arrangement complementing the yellow and blue afternoon tea setting. Place a small piece of wet floral foam inside the bowl. It doesn't need to be secured as the arrangement is small and the materials light. Begin with some small sprigs of ivy on the lower outside edge. Add a few garden snippets such as euphorbia and berries, followed by freesias and narcissus. Fill any gaps with short pieces of greenery. As a final touch, take two long pieces of fine-leafed ivy. Strip the leaves off the ends, leaving leaves in the centre only. With the first piece spike one end into the lower edge of the arrangement, and the other end on the direct opposite side of the arrangement, making a hoop. Do the same at right angles to the first with the other long piece, creating a hooped 'cage' right over the top to look a bit like two handles.

153

CUCUMBER SANDWICHES

MAKES 32

**16 slices sandwich-cut brown or
 white bread
soft butter or margarine
1 telegraph cucumber, very thinly sliced
 (leave skin on)
salt and freshly ground black pepper**

Butter the bread slices sparingly, sprinkle with salt and pepper. Layer over the sliced cucumber and sandwich together. Cut off the crusts and cut each sandwich into four. Keep covered with a damp muslin or tea-towel until serving.

EGG AND CRESS FINGER SANDWICHES

MAKES 30

**20 slices sandwich-cut brown
 or white bread
soft butter or margarine
salt and freshly ground black pepper
4 hard-boiled eggs, finely chopped
150 g spreadable cream cheese
1 teaspoon mild curry powder
2 cups (approx) mustard cress
 sprouts or watercress leaves**

Butter the bread slices sparingly and sprinkle with salt and pepper. With a fork mash the egg, cream cheese and curry powder and spread evenly onto 10 slices of bread. Layer with the sprouts or watercress leaves and lay the top slices of bread on top. Cut off the crusts and cut each sandwich into 3 fingers. Keep covered with damp muslin or tea-towel until ready to serve.

OPPOSITE PAGE: *A host of golden daffodils – ideal for a golden wedding anniversary. This wire basket is a holder for pot plants but why not use it as a vase? Here I have used three old clay flowerpots. Leave a little dirt on them for authenticity, and put plastic drink cups of water inside them. I used so many flowers that I did not need wire to hold the stems – they propped one another up. Cut the stems of the daffodils at an angle so they don't seal onto the bottom of the container. Make them just long enough that they fit snugly in a posy shape above the pot level. Allow them to face in different directions as they do in the garden. Add a few spiky leaves, such as daffodil or narcissus, to create a garden-picked look. Keep this design to just one type and colour of flower for maximum effect.*

155

LEMON SUGAR CRUST LOAF

extra sugar for sprinkling
peel of 1 lemon (peel off with a potato peeler, avoiding the pith)
1 cup sugar
4 eggs
1 cup flour
½ teaspoon baking powder

Preheat the oven to 180°C. Well grease a 12 x 23 cm loaf tin, then sprinkle it with a little sugar. In a food processor place the lemon peel and 1 cup sugar. Process until the sugar is oily and yellow and the peel very finely ground. With an electric mixer beat the eggs until pale and fluffy. Slowly add the lemon sugar, then fold in the sifted flour and baking powder. Pour into the greased and sugared loaf tin. Sprinkle some extra sugar over the top of the loaf. Bake for 35–40 minutes until the top is golden and crunchy and the loaf is cooked through. Cool on a wire rack, and slice when cool.

Tip: This loaf is also great toasted the next day.

LEMON BUTTER

MAKES 2 CUPS

2 cups caster sugar
125 g butter, cubed
4 eggs
juice and grated rind of 4 juicy lemons
  (Villa Franca or Yenben lemons have the best flavour)

Place all ingredients in a glass or microwave-safe bowl and whisk well. Cook on high for 1 minute, whisk well, then cook in bursts of about 40 seconds, whisking in between, until thick and creamy (about 5 minutes in total). Cool and store in a covered container in the fridge. When ready to serve, spoon into pastry cases. (See recipe page 14.)

Lavender, mauve and ice blue are lovely colours to use for a silver wedding anniversary. They look good placed against silver and white accessories. Jo's choice of silver foil cup cake holders (see page 161) add to the theme. This lovely lavender posy is made of lavender, green and black berries of pittosporum, ivy, angelica and Cobaea scandens. (Its cup flowers begin fresh green, turning to mauve and deep purple with a beautiful green calyx. Unfortunately the plant is regarded as a pest in some areas.)

I began the posy with a cluster of lavender stems (all at the same height), and a few sprigs of ivy and angelica. I surrounded these with Cobaea flowers, making sure the heads were facing upwards. I repeated another outer 'layer' of all the materials until I had a mounded posy. The posy is really just tightly massed flower heads, interspersed with greenery and fringed with large leaves.

The posy is edged with ivy, and I've secured the stems high up with a rubber band, using ice-green ribbon and another ribbon in shades of green for trimming.

LAVENDER SHORTBREAD

MAKES 24 PIECES

250 g butter, softened
³/₄ cup lavender-scented icing sugar (see below)
¹/₂ cup cornflour
1¹/₂ cups flour

Preheat the oven to 150°C. Beat the butter and icing sugar until creamy. Mix in the cornflour and flour. On a floured surface roll into a sausage-shaped log and slice into rounds, or roll flat and press out with a round cookie cutter. Carefully place on a greased or baking-paper-lined oven tray. Prick with a fork. Bake for 25–30 minutes, until the shortbread is pale but crisp. Cool on a wire rack and store in an airtight container.

LAVENDER-SCENTED ICING SUGAR

6 tablespoons dried lavender flowers
3 vanilla beans
1 kg icing sugar

Dry a bunch of fresh lavender for 2–3 days, then snip off the flower heads into a piece of muslin or linen. Place the vanilla beans on top of the flowers and roll up and secure with a rubber band. Fill a sealable container (such as an ice-cream container) with the icing sugar and press the muslin parcel into the middle, making sure it is completely covered with icing sugar. Store for 3–4 weeks, shaking the container every couple of days. Discard the parcel and pour sugar into a glass storage jar. Label attractively.

> **Tips:** This subtly scented sugar can be added to baked goods such as light sponge cakes, as well as meringues, whipped cream and confectionery. It is perfect for our delicate melt-in-the-mouth shortbread. In a glass jar it keeps indefinitely and makes a wonderful gift.
>
> Other scented sugars can be made with cinnamon sticks, vanilla pods, selections of whole spices, citrus peel and rose petals.

VIOLET CUPCAKES

MAKES 12

125 g butter, softened
³/₄ cup caster sugar
1 teaspoon vanilla essence

2 eggs
1¹/₂ cups self-raising flour
¹/₄ cup milk

Preheat the oven to 190°C. In a medium-sized bowl using an electric mixer beat together the butter and caster sugar. Add the vanilla. Beat in the eggs, then the flour and milk. Spoon into 12 paper cases set in deep muffin tins. Bake for 20–25 minutes until golden. Cool in the cases on a wire rack.

FROSTING

50 g butter, softened
1¹/₂–2 cups icing sugar
1–2 tablespoons milk

1–2 drops pink or lilac food
colouring (or pink and blue
mixed)

Beat the butter and icing sugar together, adding milk as necessary to give a soft, spreadable consistency. Add food colouring to the desired shade. Spread over the cakes and place a sugared violet on top of each.

SUGARED VIOLETS

1 egg white
12 fresh violet flowers

¹/₂ cup caster sugar

Lightly beat the egg white just to a soft, frothy consistency (not stiff peaks). Carefully immerse the flowers in the frothy egg white. A fine paintbrush is handy to help coat the delicate petals. Sprinkle a fine coating of caster sugar over the flowers and allow to dry for 30 minutes. These can be prepared 24 hours ahead and kept in an airtight container (but not in the fridge).

MINI CHOCOLATE ECLAIRS

MAKES 20

**1 cup water
60 g butter
1 cup flour
4 eggs**

Place the water and butter in a small saucepan. Slowly bring to the boil, ensuring that the butter melts before the water boils. When the mixture is boiling remove it from the heat, add the flour all at once and beat with a wooden spoon until the mixture forms a paste and leaves the sides of the pan. Transfer it to a large mixing bowl and cool slightly – about 5 minutes. Add the eggs one at a time and beat well after each addition. The mixture will be thick, smooth and shiny. Place the mixture in a piping or ziplock bag fitted with a plain nozzle, and pipe little fingers of mixture onto an oven tray lined with baking paper. Bake at 200°C for 30 minutes until risen and golden (don't open the oven during this time). Pierce each eclair with the point of a sharp knife and return to the oven to dry out further for 5 minutes. Cool completely on a wire rack. Split the sides of each eclair open and fill with whipped cream. Spread the top with chocolate icing or melted chocolate.

ICING

**1 cup icing sugar
2 tablespoons cocoa
25 g butter, melted
boiling water**

Mix the icing sugar and cocoa with the melted butter and enough boiling water to form a smooth, spreadable paste.

COFFEE DATE SLICE

MAKES 36 PIECES

**2 eggs
1 cup dates, finely chopped
1 cup brown sugar
1½ cups flour
2 teaspoons baking powder
175 g butter (melted)
½ cup milk
1 tablespoon sweetened coffee essence**

Preheat the oven to 150°C. Beat the eggs, add the remaining ingredients and mix well. Spread into a well-greased or baking-paper-lined slice or sponge roll tray. Bake for 30 minutes. Cool in the tray. Ice with Coffee Icing, then cut into squares or fingers.

COFFEE ICING

**2 cups icing sugar
25 g butter, melted
1 tablespoon sweetened coffee essence
boiling water**

Mix all ingredients together, adding enough boiling water to form a smooth, spreadable icing.

OPPOSITE PAGE: *Golden-edged plates and daffodils to mark a golden anniversary. The finger food includes pastry cases (see recipe page 14) filled with prawns on a bed of sour cream and topped with a tiny sprig of parsley (bottom right), Mini Chocolate Eclairs (top right) and Coffee Date Slices (bottom left).*

BABY CELEBRATIONS

Baby showers, the return from hospital, christenings, naming ceremonies – whatever the focus for your celebration, everyone wants to toast the new arrival.

We've suggested some special ways to wet the baby's head and some recipes as light and gentle as the new arrival. Tradition insists on pale blue and pink, but we also have some different colour decorating ideas, which are a welcome, refreshing change.

A novel idea for an afternoon tea table decoration to celebrate the naming of a new baby. Forget about a flummery of pink and blue – cream and lemon are a lovely alternative. Here I have made a teddy bear tree which could also be recycled for baby's room later. Any tall container will do. This one is lightweight zinc, so I've put stones into the bottom for stability. Gather branches, ensuring they are varying shapes and sizes that will look good in any direction. These are wedged into the stones (top up with stones or crushed paper if your branches are not stable enough). The decorations are resin teddy bears. (Actually they are Christmas tree decorations but who's to know? Always keep a eye out for tree decorations of a general nature.) I have hung them at intervals and tied on a wired lemon ribbon bow for extra effect. Stuff crushed lemon tissue paper into the container for the finishing touch. Quick and easy, but effective.

COCONUT ANGEL FOOD CAKE

SERVES 8–10

1 cup flour
1 1/2 cups sugar
12 egg whites
1/2 teaspoon cream of tartar
2 teaspoons vanilla essence
1 teaspoon coconut essence
1 cup coarse-thread coconut (toasted in the microwave)

Preheat the oven to 190°C. Sift the flour and half the sugar into a bowl and set aside. Place the egg whites and cream of tartar in a bowl and beat until soft peaks form. Gradually add the remaining sugar and beat until thick and glossy. Fold the vanilla, coconut essence and flour mixture into the egg whites. Pour this mixture into a non-greased 23 cm angel food cake tin and bake for 35–40 minutes, or until the cake is cooked when tested with a skewer. Invert the tin and allow the cake to cool upside down (very important). When it is cool run a knife around the edge of the tin to release the cake. Slice the cake into two or three layers with a serrated bread knife. Spread Creamy Coconut Frosting between the layers and over the top Sprinkle with the toasted coconut, gently pressing it into the frosting to help it stick.

CREAMY COCONUT FROSTING

100 g butter, softened
1 teaspoon coconut essence
3 cups (approx) icing sugar

Beat all ingredients together to a soft, spreadable consistency, adding extra icing sugar if required.

Tip: Use the spare egg yolks for ice-cream, Béarnaise or Hollandaise Sauce or scrambled eggs.

MERINGUES

MAKES 24 HALVES

3 egg whites
1 cup caster sugar
2 teaspoons cornflour

½ teaspoon vanilla
1 teaspoon malt vinegar

Preheat the oven to 120°C. Beat the egg whites until stiff, then slowly – a teaspoonful at a time – beat in the caster sugar. Continue beating for about 10 minutes until the mixture is thick and glossy. Beat in the cornflour, vanilla and vinegar. Spoon the mixture into a ziplock plastic bag or piping bag fitted with a star nozzle. Pipe out small meringues onto a baking-paper-lined oven tray. Bake for 45 minutes until crisp and dry. They should lift off the paper easily when cooked. Cool on a wire rack and store in an airtight container. To serve, fill two meringue halves with whipped cream and Lemon Butter (page 156) or Passionfruit Butter (page 170).

LEFT: *Isn't this exquisite? A tiny wire-mesh pram is lined with dried green moss. I've left space inside to snugly press a small rectangular plastic margarine container, which holds a block of wet floral foam. Miniature pink rosebuds are cut very short and arranged tightly together in the foam. Make sure you use all the green buds too, and add a few wisps of moss in between some of the flowers to break up the carpet of colour and add a new texture.*

PASSIONFRUIT BUTTER

MAKES 2 CUPS

pulp of 12 juicy passionfruit
100 g butter, cut into cubes

2 eggs
3/4 cup caster sugar

Place all ingredients in a glass or microwave-safe bowl and stir well. Microwave on 100% power for 1 minute, then whisk well. Continue to cook in bursts of about 40 seconds, whisking in between, until thick and creamy (about 5 minutes altogether). Cool and store in a covered container in the fridge.

> **Tip:** You can use passionfruit butter on toast, crumpets and muffins or to fill cakes, tarts and meringues or top pavlovas. Yum!

ABOVE: *Fabric is an attractive alternative to wrapping paper for a baby gift. Pink cotton gingham is perfect for baby Jessie and is fastened with nappy pins. The trimming is made from the letter beads used to identify baby on arrival in hospital.*

OPPOSITE PAGE: *Hot orange crêpe paper with scarlet, orange and yellow cheque ribbon creates a stunning baby parcel, instead of the usual pastel pinks and blues. The tiny wooden pram trim is a recycled Christmas tree decoration.*

MINT JULEPS

1 cup sugar
½ cup water
bourbon
crushed ice
mint leaves and sprigs
iced soda water or mineral water

First make a simple sugar syrup by dissolving the sugar in the water, stirring over a gentle heat until dissolved. Keep this chilled syrup in a screw-top jar in the fridge. To make the Mint Juleps pour 2 parts bourbon and 1 part sugar syrup over crushed ice and bruised mint leaves. Top up with iced soda or mineral water and garnish with fresh mint sprigs.

> **Tip:** Mint Juleps are traditionally served in silver cups, so old silver christening mugs are a splendid substitute.

WATERMELON
SLUSHY

SERVES 4

½ cup water
½ cup caster sugar
1 small or ½ large watermelon, seeds and skin removed
juice and grated rind of 2 limes

Combine the water and caster sugar in a small saucepan or microwave-safe jug. Bring to the boil, stirring until the sugar has dissolved. Cool. Purée the melon in a blender. Combine with the lime juice and rind and sugar syrup. Freeze in a plastic container (eg, an ice-cream container). To serve, cut the frozen watermelon juice into chunks and whiz briefly in a blender until slushy. Serve with wedges of lime in glasses.

YOUTH CELEBRATIONS

Having a horde of young people over may be daunting, but it doesn't have to be hard work. Choosing a vivid theme or a different location can make the event memorable, be it for end-of-term parties, leaving school, or celebrating sweet 16, reaching 18, or the more traditional 21.

Here are two suggestions to make the event stress-free: a colourful Mexican theme to get them dancing away excess energy; and the special picnic (where you have no worries about limited room, maximum mess or annoying the neighbours). The picnic could be out in the country, on a beach or even in your back garden: let them go wild in the wild!

A spicy colour combination to match the spicy food. We've provided filling food but nothing that requires a formal seating arrangement or elaborate preparation.

175

CHILLI BEANS FOR A CROWD

SERVES 14–16

¼ cup oil
4 large onions peeled and roughly chopped
3 teaspoons chilli seasoning mix
6 x 400 g (approx) cans kidney beans
3 x 400 g cans peeled tomatoes in juice, crushed
1 x 375 g jar thick and chunky salsa
sweet chilli sauce (optional)
sour cream to garnish
coriander or parsley sprigs to garnish

Heat the oil in a large saucepan, add the chopped onions and cook for 3–4 minutes. Add the chilli seasoning, rinsed kidney beans, canned tomatoes and the salsa. Mix well, chopping up any large pieces of tomato. Simmer for 10 minutes to heat thoroughly and allow the flavours to develop. Taste and check the seasoning, adding some chilli sauce if desired. Serve in small cups or bowls garnished with sour cream and a sprig of coriander or parsley.

TOASTED CHEESE MUFFINS

MAKES 12

2 cups flour
4 teaspoons baking powder
½ teaspoon salt
1 cup grated tasty cheese
1 egg
¼ cup oil
1¼ cups milk
extra grated cheese for sprinkling

Preheat the oven to 200°C. Stir the first seven ingredients together in a large bowl, just lightly mixing to combine. Don't overwork the mixture or the muffins will be tough and heavy. Spoon the mixture, which should be fairly runny and pourable, into deep non-stick muffin tins. Sprinkle with a few shreds of grated cheese. Bake for 15–20 minutes until golden brown.

QUESADILLAS

MAKES 40 BITE-SIZE PORTIONS

8 soft flour tortillas
2 cups grated cheese
4 teaspoons sweet chilli sauce

Spread 4 tortillas with chilli sauce, as if you are buttering toast. Sprinkle each with $\frac{1}{2}$ cup grated cheese and press a second unspread tortilla on top. Microwave individually for $1\frac{1}{2}$ minutes to melt the cheese (you can also do this in a large frying pan or on a barbecue plate). Cool for a minute or two and cut each into 10 wedges with scissors. Serve warm.

*W*arm rich colours and hot spicy nibbles – who could resist? A line-up of vibrant cyclamen-coloured tin buckets hold sunflowers, chillies dried on their stems and pink-coloured Fijian fireplant leaves. A block of wet floral foam is placed inside each bucket. Six small sunflower heads with their own foliage are spiked in, and a few stems of chillies (you could wire single chillies onto satay sticks for a similar effect). The lower leaves of the Fijian fireplant are cut short and added as a collar to complete the arrangement. The pillar candles are in the six bold colours of the enamel dinner plates with matching napkins. The candles are set among mandarin foliage, fruit and chillies scattered on the table top.

CHEESE SCONES

MAKES 10–12

75 g butter
1¼ cups milk
3 cups self-raising flour
½ teaspoon salt
1 cup (or a good handful) grated cheese

Preheat the oven to 220°C. Heat the butter and milk in the microwave until the butter is melted and milk is quite hot (hot bath temperature). Add the flour, salt and grated cheese and mix to a smooth, soft dough. With floured hands and working quickly, shape into small balls or cut out rounds with a 4–5 cm cookie cutter. Place on a floured tray, quite close together. Brush the tops with milk and if desired sprinkle a few shreds of grated cheese over. Bake for about 15 minutes until golden brown. Cool on a wire rack covered with a clean tea-towel.

> **Tips:** This is such a handy recipe to have in your repertoire – use it as a 'quick bread' with soups and salads or for impromptu morning and afternoon teas. Fancy small shaped scones get more brownie points than big hunky doorstops. Scones reheat beautifully in the microwave, even the next day.

BEER BREAD

3 cups flour
3 teaspoons baking powder
1 teaspoon salt
1 can beer (rinse out the can with water to make the volume up to
**   400 ml – don't use low-alcohol beer)**
1 handful (about ½ cup) grated cheese

Preheat the oven to 200°C. Mix the flour, baking powder, salt and beer in a large bowl until well combined. Tip into a large 21 x 12 cm non-stick or well-greased loaf tin (or use 2 smaller 8 x 15 cm tins). Sprinkle the top with grated cheese. Bake the large loaf for 50–60 minutes or the two little loaves for 30–40 minutes until golden brown. Tip out and cool on a wire rack before slicing.

> **Tips:** I had to include my famous beer bread recipe, which is just so quick and handy to whiz up when you need bread in a hurry. The local hot bread shop could go out of business when you master this one. This bread keeps well and also makes excellent toast.

OPPOSITE PAGE: *There's nothing like a picnic done with flair. This tempting basket is lined with huge chunky linen tea-towels. Add a scented as well as decorative touch by binding fresh herbs together to create borders on each side inside the towel. Begin with long straight pieces of rosemary that fit along the length and width of the basket. I then used green cotton (or you could use fine florist's wire) to tie in sprigs of bay and thyme evenly along the rosemary lengths. It's a great way to enhance the yummy warm bread.*

CAMEMBERT, CHICKEN & ROAST PEPPER PICNIC PIE

SERVES 6–8

3 sheets pre-rolled puff pastry
6 boneless chicken breasts, skinned
1 tablespoon olive oil
2 small rounds of camembert cheese (2 x 100 g approx)
8 roast pepper halves (can be bought from the deli)
1 cup grated parmesan cheese
1 teaspoon dried thyme
egg wash (1 egg yolk beaten with 1 tablespoon cold water)
3 tablespoons extra grated parmesan cheese

Preheat the oven to 180°C. Grease a large (23 x 15 x 6 cm) loaf tin and line the base with baking paper. Line with one layer of the puff pastry, joining sheets as necessary and leaving a good fold-over edge on one side. Beat the chicken breasts flat between 2 sheets of plastic clingfilm. Heat the oil in a large pan and gently fry the chicken breasts until just cooked through – there is no need to colour the meat. Cool slightly. Slice the camembert thinly. Layer up the chicken, peppers, grated parmesan, camembert and thyme. Fold the pastry over the filling and crimp the edges. Brush with egg wash and sprinkle with the extra parmesan. Bake for 45 minutes. Cool in the tin, then ease the cold pie out of the tin with a knife. Peel off the base paper and wrap the pie in foil or clingfilm and chill until ready to serve.

ABOVE: *Citronella tea-light candles could be a welcome addition to your picnic if you are dining in mosquito territory. Cut a neat hole in an apple (or other firm fruit such as an orange) and wedge the tea-light down a little below the flesh level. Great for barbecues or even indoors.*

THE FLORAL DECORATOR'S PANTRY

It is a good idea to develop an eye for interesting natural items while you're out walking and to gather things when you see them.

I have a cupboard full of bits and pieces that I bring out when the mood strikes and can later put away for another day. I also hoard candles, buying them when I see something special or find good deals.

A decorator's pantry, complete with hoarded candles, my invaluable candle-holders (centre of top and middle shelves), used in so many displays, containers picked up from anywhere and everywhere, cones and other material foraged from country and garden, and boxes and tools.

Conifer cones last for ever when dried and there are many fascinating varieties. Dry them in an airy place and then store for use at winter solstice or Christmas. Other plants' seeds are interesting too. Magnolia, alder and idesia all have seeds that dry and keep.

Moss is a beautiful accessory. Dry it – or buy it – and use it again and again. It is great for hiding the mechanics of an arrangement, or as a textured surface or a lovely foil along an edge. Take care if you are out gathering it – some of our mosses are protected. In fact, you need to be careful when gathering anything – don't pillage the countryside. Observe the rules that apply to reserves, parks and private land.

Lichen-encrusted twigs can be kept to include in fresh arrangements or as a branch on which to hang decorations. Bare silver birch branches are a treasure. Gather them in the winter, then twist into round wreath shapes for use at Christmas. They are also lovely entwined around a candelabra, or tied into a rustic tangly bow. Silver birch branches are pliable and do not become as brittle as some other branches when they are dry.

The water's edge is another treasure trove. Shells, stones and pumice will all come in handy. Chestnuts, acorns and walnuts are wonderful for winter and autumn decorations. Dried chillies add a splash of colour and will keep for ages, and so will some gourds. Feathers never date. Keep a supply on hand for a wacky arrangement. Don't discard candles that have burnt down a fair way. They may look past their best but a collection of them in a rustic container (even an old cake tin) and used en masse is surprisingly effective.

OPPOSITE PAGE: *Wrapping, tying and trimming parcels is an integral part of gift giving. I love natural materials and colours and enjoy searching out things like unusual ties and trims with a difference.*

Try 'toasting' paper to give the appearance of ageing. Use a sheet of strong, white paper and toast it very lightly under the grill. Take great care not to set it alight! Wrap your parchment parcel, tie it with gold and red ribbon and add a blob of sealing wax. Hand-made paper is often in earthy natural shades. Look for some cheap domestic trimmings such as upholstery tape, webbing and string. Trims can range from cones, cinnamon sticks and dried leaves to a voluptuous full-blown garden rose.

Some boxes can make a stunning present in their own right – such as the Shaker box and the old collar box on page 134. Just tie them with a stunning bow. Cigar and chocolate boxes are sometimes far too beautiful to wrap. Just tie a lovely ribbon around these, too.

A gift of flowers does not always need paper around it. Try edging it with large leaves. They make a lovely collar as well as protecting the flowers. Home-made preserves or sweets can be given a special twist by presenting them in a tissue-lined gift box with a hand-made card or in a pretty basket that can be used again.

OTHER FLORAL DECORATOR'S PANTRY ITEMS

- Artificial apples or berries can be used in all kinds of arrangements.
- Artificial grasses (used on pages 10 and 130).
- Christmas decorations can be kept for generations.
- Secateurs to be used for plant material only.
- Another pair of cutters for wire.
- Terracotta flower pots and any unusual containers I find in junk shops, church fêtes, markets and auctions.
- Plastic ice-cream, yoghurt or take-away containers and heavy polythene are useful as liners.
- Florist's spray to colour and preserve fresh flowers. I use green spray for moss that has turned brown.
- A hot-glue gun or glue from craft shops.
- Floristry wire (some florists will sell it to you in different gauges).
- String, raffia and ribbons.
- Floral foam comes in two forms – one to soak in water for fresh arrangements and one to use for permanent designs. I prefer crumpled chicken wire (5 cm mesh) in water for fresh flowers, but foam does have its place.

Candles are associated with celebration, ritual and joyful times. Intermingled here with other materials they add a festive note. The tall candelabra at the back has had a few long trails of ivy entwined around each branch – elegant ivy is wonderful for tarting up candle-holders! The urns each hold a pillar candle kept upright with a few stones and trimmed with a twig of small-leafed ivy. The tiny pots in front have a short pillar candle encased in moss. Be careful not to let the flame near the dry moss. The fat triple-wicked candle on the bottom right-hand side is set on an old lead plate and decorated with a few stones.

The bold arrangement has an exotic container made of spun bamboo. It holds a plastic pot plant tray stuffed with two brick-sized blocks of wet floral foam. The three pillar candles are set in the centre (remember, odd numbers look best). Leave a gap between them or you could have a bonfire! Add short-cut bold flowers such as sunflowers to the foam, placed at slightly different angles (or they'll look like a row of traffic lights). Intersperse them with fruit such as oranges or apples. (A word from the wise: Try to use candles in such a way that if they should drip wax it will be collected within a holder and not leak onto linen or a precious table top.)

CANDLE TIPS

Before lighting a candle for the first time, trim the wick to 1.5 cm. Then light it and allow it to burn for about 3 hours. Snuff the candle out after this time, avoiding damage to the wick. Whenever it is lit hereafter, the candle should melt within itself rather than drip down the sides.

If necessary, trim the wick again before re-lighting. Long wicks can burn a hole through the wall of the candle, causing drips. They also tend to smoke. If possible, keep lit candles away from draughts, ceiling fans, and air conditioning. These conditions will also cause a candle to drip.

Large candles form a lot of liquid wax so take care not to knock them. If wax spills on any cloth, allow it to set. Then put the cloth in the freezer (yes!), and when the wax is brittle you should be able to chip it off. If the freezer is not an option, scrape off the excess wax from the fabric once it has set, then iron the stain through brown or absorbent paper. This should blot up any stain, but if any remains it may be bleached out of white cotton or linen, otherwise take the item to a dry cleaner for professional removal.

Take care when using candles around flammable decorations and never leave lit candles unattended. Replace the candle before it burns too far down.

OPPOSITE ABOVE: *Candles look lovely set among flowers. Here I have simply pushed the candle into the wet floral foam. (Make sure you know exactly where you want the candle before pushing it in – once the hole is made there's no going back!)*

This wire flowerpot holder holds two old terracotta flowerpots into which I have put plastic yoghurt pots. There's no need to spend a fortune on flowers. I bought two bunches of ranunculas and *supplemented them with garden-picked snippets. Start with blocks of wet floral foam pressed into the yoghurt pots and add the candles. Poke some large leaves into the foam around the outsides of the pots, then add small bits and pieces of greenery. Here I have used ivy tips, euphorbia, clivia berries, variegated thyme and scented geranium.*

Cut the flower heads short (roses would be good, too) and place the largest blooms nearest the centre for balance. Use all the *buds too – at a longer length than the flowers – along with the greenery they will give the arrangement a garden-picked look. Lastly, pop in some dried green moss to fill in any gaps and give another texture. Moss really is a must in your decorative pantry! You can replace the candles if the flowers outlast them. This design could be given a lovely Christmas twist by using red candles, greenery and a few small dried cones.*

BELOW: *A glass flower holder creates an 'aquarium' for stones, shells and a four-wick candle. You could use a shallow plate or a round glass vase with a round candle. Put stones (or small shells) in an even level over the bottom of the vase. Place the candle on top and then arrange a few shells and starfish around the candle. This design could also have water in it and a few floating flower heads.*

TIPS FOR CONDITIONING FLOWERS

- Re-cut flower and foliage stems before putting into water. Cut stems at an angle. It gives the stem a larger area through which to drink and also means that the stem cannot seal onto the bottom of the container. Tepid water is a good reviver.
- Stand flowers in a bucket of water, preferably overnight, in a cool place, before arranging them.
- Split or crush woody stems.
- Remove any bottom leaves that will be below water level.
- If possible, change the water in your vase every one or two days.
- If flowers flag after they have been arranged, pull them out of the arrangement and repeat the care process, then pop them back.

One final note: if using flowers alongside food, ensure the flowers are not poisonous. If in doubt, choose flowers that are edible, such as roses, marigolds, nasturtiums, violets, cymbidium orchids or herbs. It's a good idea to keep food away from floral foam, too.

ACKNOWLEDGEMENTS

Special thanks are given to the following for their assistance in putting this book together:

Acland Holdings
Amanda Herbert
Baran de Bordeaux
Bedingfields
Bloomsbury Galleries
Brenda Legg
Claire Bennett
Colour and Movement
Diana Hill
Donatus Heinrichs
Eddy Sheath
Eve Hill
Fay Wellwood
French Country Collections
Gen and Gordon Hogg
Grant Allen
Harriet Allan
Heather Jones
Jillian Bashford Evers

John Walsh
Maddison's Party Hire
Maree O'Neill
Maytime
Mike O'Donnell
Natalie Hoelen
National Candles
Nest
Paul Verdon
Penny Milne
Peter Sharp
Sandy Hayward
Sheryl Palmer
Shirley Anderson
Tabletops Hire
Terence O'Neill-Joyce
The Deacon Family
The Front Room
Tony Verdon

INDEX OF DECORATIVE IDEAS

INDEX OF RECIPES